ADVANCE PRAISE FOR *WOLF WARS*

"Hank Fischer has been a steadfast anchor in that ever changing sea of emotion, noise, and ego surrounding wolf politics. We're fortunate to have an accurate account from a grounded activist who's been at the center of wolf reintroduction from the very beginning."

—Jim Brandenburg—
Author of *Brother Wolf: A Forgotten Promise*

"Hank Fischer's entertaining, tell-it-like-it-is chronicle of the 20-year struggle to restore wolves to Yellowstone is must reading for anyone interested in wolves, endangered species, the environment, or biopolitics."

—L. David Mech—
**Author of *The Wolf: The Ecology and Behavior
of an Endangered Species***

"Fischer's tight and clean writing, full of wit, intimate detail, despair, joy, and frustration, gives us a revealing tale with the rarest of conclusions in the wildlife restoration business—a happy ending."

—John D. Varley—
**National Park Service, Director of the Yellowstone Center
for Resources, Yellowstone National Park**

MORE PRAISE FOR *WOLF WARS*

"Hank Fischer offers an insightful and thoughtful insider's view of the long and difficult journey of wolf recovery in the West. Mr. Fischer's own dedication and ingenuity were principal ingredients in the success of the project he skillfully chronicles in *Wolf Wars*."

—Renée Askins—
Executive Director of The Wolf Fund

"Hank Fischer has a gift for telling a great story about the most polarized and emotional wildlife restoration project in North America. He was at the center throughout this debate. His insight provides anyone interested in wolves with a fascinating behind-the-scenes look at how political and public pressure finally resulted in wolves being returned to Yellowstone, the world's first national park."

—Ed Bangs—
Gray Wolf Reintroduction Project Leader
for U.S. Fish and Wildlife Service

WOLF WARS

The Remarkable Inside Story
of the Restoration of Wolves
to Yellowstone

BY HANK FISCHER

FALCON™

Front cover photo by Daniel J. Cox.
Back cover photo courtesy of U.S. Fish and Wildlife Service.

Design, typesetting, and other prepress work by
Falcon Press, Helena, Montana.
Printed in U.S.A.
ISBN: 1-56044-352-9 $12.95 softcover
ISBN: 1-56044-351-0 $19.95 hardcover
Library of Congress Catalog Number: 95-60292

For Carol, Andrew, and Kit Fischer,
the ones who matter most

F O R E W O R D

In 1968, when I finished the manuscript of my book *The Wolf: The Ecology and Behavior of an Endangered Species*, the gray wolf had just been listed as an endangered species in the lower forty-eight states; the Soviet Union had declared its war on wolves; poisoning was still widespread across Canada; and the purity of the red wolf, which inhabits the southeastern United States, was rapidly being eroded by an influx of coyote genes.

Between public hatred and government extermination, wolves had disappeared from one-third to one-half of their former range, which originally included almost all the landmass of the Northern Hemisphere above twenty degrees latitude (which runs through Mexico City and Bombay, India). They were gone from much of western Europe and the more populated areas of Asia as well as from most of Mexico and the contiguous United States. If the wolf had any friends, it wasn't clear who they were.

But much has changed since then. In the past twenty-five years, environmental awareness has burgeoned like never before. Earth Day was born, Congress passed the Endangered Species Act, and "ecology" has become a household word as organizations like Defenders of Wildlife and the World Wildlife Fund have fostered a remarkable new environmental movement.

The wolf's repopulation of the northern parts of the lower forty-eight states, now well under way, will stand as one of the primary conservation achievements of the twentieth century. Society will have come full circle and corrected its grave overreaction to its main mammalian competitor. Maybe not quite full circle. If we have learned anything from this ordeal, it is that the best way to ensure continued wolf survival is, ironically enough, not to protect wolves completely. If we carefully regulate wolf populations instead of overprotecting them, we can prevent a second wave of wolf hysteria, a backlash that could lead once again to persecution.

The citizens of this nation have responded to an age of shame, taking extraordinary measures to right a blatant wrong done by their forebears. Wolves are being returned to Yellowstone National Park, where the government long ago wiped them out at the public's behest. These magnificent creatures similarly are being reintroduced to central Idaho.

Hank Fischer knows the story well. His knowledge, however, is not just that of a highly interested bystander. He was an important player in the restoration of wolves. As the Northern Rockies representative of Defenders of Wildlife, a long-standing advisor to the Northern Rocky Mountain Wolf Recovery Team, and an active environmentalist with a keen eye for the practical side of wolf recovery, Hank contributed significantly to moderating the regional anti-wolf climate.

Who else would have thought of whisking prominent western livestock representatives to Minnesota to see for themselves how well the state's ranchers coexist with wolves? Hank knew that the trip would produce no converts. But he also knew that providing firsthand, accurate information to opinion leaders just might moderate their rhetoric. It would also show a willingness by environmentalists to go the extra mile in considering livestock producers' concerns.

Hank had another ingenious idea: using private funds to pay stockgrowers for livestock losses to wolves. At his urging, Defenders set up a $100,000 Wolf Compensation Fund. By contributing to the fund, citizens can play an active role in wolf restoration. Certainly, this program has greatly helped blunt the livestock industry's criticism of wolf restoration. In Minnesota, "Put your money where your mouth is" had long been a challenge livestock growers hurled at environmentalists trying to protect the wolf. Hank saw to it that wolf advocates could do just that.

Hank even went himself one better. Soon, Defenders offered $5,000 to anyone in the West who let wolves raise pups on his land. It worked. A pack of wolves produced a litter on a ranch along the eastern front of Montana's Rockies, and in 1994, Defenders cut the landowner a check.

Many people have contributed to wolf restoration and the environmental revolution it represents. Hank Fischer is prominent among them, and I am pleased to be able to pay him tribute. His book helps document the roles of many others working toward the same goals and reveals the extreme dedication, diligence, persistence, and ingenuity that were necessary to the task.

Although wolf restoration can never compensate for all the environmental havoc wreaked by our own species, it is a heartening symbol of a new public vision. I hope it is also a harbinger of a more environmentally sensitive outlook by our still-emerging culture.

We have reached a great milestone in conservation, but let us not stop here. Instead, let us ensure that the new Yellowstone Park wolf population signifies not just a new appreciation for one species but also a greater resolve to respect and nourish all parts of our environment.

— *L. DAVID MECH* —

SPECIAL NOTE

It is sad but true that an important part of America's wildlife heritage, especially large mammals like wolves and bears, persists chiefly because of human tolerance. Indeed, continuing population growth and urbanization may eventually make this the dominant fact of life for most wild animals, even though this debases those species while excessively aggrandizing humankind. For better or worse, humans are now playing the godlike role of determining which species will survive and which will not, and just where and how.

But while wildlife is inevitably becoming hostage to human attitudes, humans also have much at stake. Biologists now recognize that spreading habitat degradation and species loss pose great risks to both ecology and human welfare. The very survival of our descendants will depend upon maintaining the basic ecosystem services performed by the countless living things—plants, insects, and other invertebrates, tiny rodents, birds, bats, and microbes as well as larger creatures—that are integral to maintaining life on Earth.

For most of human history, there has been no need for concern about sustaining the intricate processes of nature. But because of relentless human population growth and modern technology's capacity for altering the natural world, our planet for the first time since the extinction of the dinosaurs sixty-five million years ago is losing species faster than nature can evolve new ones. We are rapidly depleting vital living resources upon which we depend. Extinctions are now occurring literally thousands of times faster than the creation of new species. Harvard evolutionary biologist Edward O. Wilson estimates that by the time a child born today reaches his or her thirtieth birthday, one of every five current species on the Earth will be either doomed or already extinct. After that, if the present trend continues, the prospect will worsen.

Although this is the future that science currently forecasts, it need not happen. But if our progeny are to have a better prospect, we must revise our attitude toward nature's other life forms. Taking our cue from the philosophy of the great conservationist Aldo Leopold, we must change from exploiters and conquerors to partners of nature.

Can humankind come to accept the idea that "the community of man" should embrace not simply our own species but all living things? Can we focus sufficiently on the welfare of future human generations and the rest of the living world, both now so dangerously dependent upon us, to develop a live-and-let-live attitude toward other species?

The answer is not yet clear. But the effort to return the wolf to Yellowstone Park should give us encouragement. The wolf, after all, has long been subjected to persecution and even hatred by humans. Yet this is changing. To many, the wolf now ranks as a special, very positive, even inspiring symbol of the animal world, of the wild, of unspoiled nature. Restoring the wolf to the nation's and the world's first national park, a place dedicated to nature conservation and appreciation, is thus doubly symbolic, a dramatic affirmation of a deepening ethic. Yellowstone Park wolf restoration will one day be regarded as a watershed in both wildlife conservation and broader human history—the time when America committed itself to a more enlightened, noble, and moral view of humanity's role in nature.

— *RODGER SCHLICKEISEN* —

PRESIDENT, DEFENDERS OF WILDLIFE

C O N T E N T S

P R O L O G U E

Often when I pass through the Roosevelt Arch, the rough-hewn stone structure spanning the original entrance to Yellowstone National Park, I'm filled with an overwhelming sense of awe and nostalgia. The park endures as one of the most culturally and historically significant places in America. It's to the United States what the Great Barrier Reef is to Australia, the Pyramids are to Egypt, the Galapagos Islands are to Ecuador. It helps define who we are as a nation and what we believe in.

The park's designation in 1872 was a miracle of foresight, early testimony to the power this landscape exerts over its visitors. The Yellowstone area had been home to Native Americans for thousands of years, but white settlers were only beginning to move into the region when Congress acted to preserve Yellowstone Park. In the 1870s, most Americans saw the West as a place to be made safe for mining, farming, grazing, and settling. They viewed this unknown wild country as a repository of material treasures, not spiritual ones. That Yellowstone became the United States' first national park when our country was in its most exploitative phase may be the truest measure of the hold this place takes on people's souls.

Yellowstone Park attracts people for different reasons. Some seek a geothermal display equaled nowhere else on earth—from sulphurous mud pots that bubble and gurgle to geysers that hiss, spit, and hurl water hundreds of feet into the sky.

The park's unique geology captivates others. The Grand Canyon of the Yellowstone River, with its rock steeples and towering waterfalls, is among the most scenic places in the West. The giant collapsed volcanic crater that forms the central part of the park is a geologic marvel.

But for many people, wildlife defines this 2.2 million-acre park. No place in North America contains a higher concentration of elk and bison. When their numbers peak in midsummer, upward of 30,000 elk and 3,500 bison roam the park.

The wildlife spectacle is as close as this hemisphere comes to Tanzania's Serengeti, but there's a significant flaw: its most significant predator—the gray wolf—has been missing for most of the twentieth century. Would the African plains be the same without the lion? Predators exert powerful evolutionary influences on their prey. As natural historian Stephen Jay Gould has suggested, natural history is largely a tale of species' adaptations to avoid predation.

One day in March 1989, the absence of wolves made an indelible impression on me. The summer before, forest fires had raced through many parts of Yellowstone Park, not only burning trees but also scorching shrubs and grasses important to wintering elk and bison. In February, a ferocious winter storm with winds gusting as high as fifty miles an hour had ripped through the Northern Rockies, dropping deep snow and driving the windchill to seventy degrees below zero. Elk, already stressed by poor nutrition, began to die in the park in huge numbers. By the end of winter, as many as 7,500 lay dead, according to National Park Service estimates. Winter was the cruelest predator of all.

The day I visited the park wasn't particularly cold, but the snow was still deep, and elk were still dying. Contorted carcasses littered the white expanse along every small drainage. Intermingled with the dead were the dying.

Would so many of these animals die, I wondered, if Yellowstone Park were still home to its most important large predator? I'd posed this question to many scientists. Some contended that the elk population was so enormous— especially in the northern part of the park—that it wouldn't be influenced much by even a fairly large number of wolves. These scientists speculated that the elk's reproductive rate might simply increase to compensate for greater predation by wolves.

Other scientists took a different view. They predicted that wolves would cause a significant decline in the elk population—perhaps on the order of 20 percent. Winter die-offs might still occur, they theorized—at least for the short term. But winterkill wouldn't be as drastic because, throughout the year, wolves would kill unfit animals before they starved or succumbed to the elements.

That same day, I hiked into an area in the northern part of the park called McMinn Bench to photograph bighorn sheep. A few years earlier, many members of the herd there had fallen victim to keratoconjunctivitis, commonly known as pinkeye. It's a highly contagious disease sometimes contracted by humans. In bighorn sheep, it causes blindness (usually temporary), a condition that can be fatal to these cliff-dwelling animals. The Park Service estimated that the outbreak claimed nearly 50 percent of the sheep population as a result of accidents or an inability to feed or find shelter.

As I watched these blocky animals cavort among the rocks, I thought about the effect wolves might have had on a herd of visually impaired sheep. The predators might have decimated such helpless prey, maybe even killed them all. Or wolves might have killed the first bighorns to contract the disease, perhaps preventing the spread of infection throughout the herd. Such are the complexities of predation.

The Roman natural historian Pliny the Elder once wrote, "Nature is to be found in her entirety nowhere more than in her smallest creatures." To appreciate his wisdom, you need only split open a decaying log and watch the complexity of activities within.

But the opposite is just as true. Large predators are "the big things that run the world," asserts Princeton University biology professor John Terborgh. He says that big carnivores create changes that ripple through natural systems, affecting all parts, large and small. Restoring wolves to Yellowstone Park would redefine the entire ecosystem, I reflected, from the elk right down to the smallest clump of bluebunch wheatgrass.

In his 1990 book, *The Kingdom*, Doug Chadwick eloquently sums up wolves' impact on other species. "I do not think it is possible to truly understand even one leg muscle of one elk in the absence of wolves. Not a single leap of a single deer, nor any traverse of any mountain goat across a winterbound cliff wall. The size and endurance of hoofed beasts on this continent; their speed, coordination and quicksilver reactions; their social structure and communication abilities—wolves sang these things into their present form."

I confess to having no greater affection for wolves than for any other creature. The one time I spotted a wolf in the wild was while circling tightly in a researcher's airplane. I don't live to hear a wolf howl split the night sky or dream of finding a wolf track in fresh snow, but I hope to experience both someday.

I've spent more than fifteen years trying, along with many other people, to restore wolves to Yellowstone Park. Why have I worked so long on behalf of a species for which I profess no special fondness? My romance is with Yellowstone Park's natural system as a whole. I'm captivated by the intricate interplay of wolves; elk; aspen; beetles; ravens; fire; weather; *and* people, the aspect of the equation all too often overlooked. All these parts—plus thousands we've yet to comprehend—working together in a random yet reciprocal way create the essence of Yellowstone Park: wildness. The circular trail of the wolf leads us there.

WOLF RECOVERY
⟶ IN THE NORTHERN ROCKIES ⟵

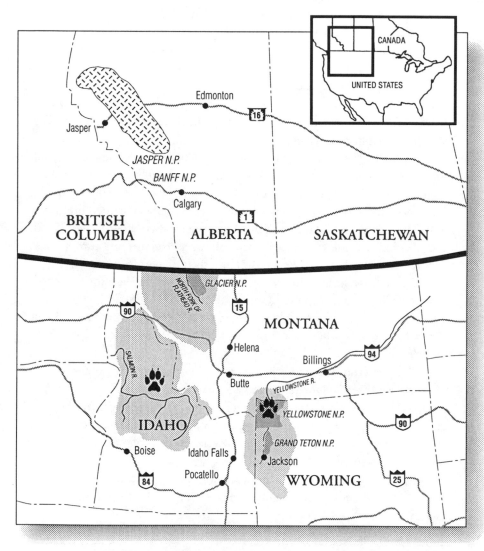

Wolf Capture Site

 Wolf Release Sites in Idaho and Yellowstone National Park

Wolf Recovery Areas in the Northern Rockies

INVASION OF THE WOLF SNATCHERS

A big black wolf with a silver streak on his throat lay quietly in a bed he'd dug in the snow, his muzzle resting on his paws. Snow sifted down and stuck to the white-flecked guard hairs on his face and neck.*

He was tired—wolf tired. The previous day and night had been strenuous for the big male and the other nine wolves that lay nearby, gnawing bones from their recent kill. As wolves go, they were unremarkable, just another pack of wolves living in the foothills of the Canadian Rockies in west-central Alberta. But on January 10, 1995, they became the most famous wolves in the world.

The big male was the leader of the pack, the alpha male. Five of the wolves were his pups, born the preceding April. Although all were approaching full size—seventy to one hundred pounds—they

---

* I've drawn from conversations with biologists and the scientific literature on wolves to construct this account of what no one knows: details about the lives of the Petite Lake wolves leading up to the day some of them were captured.

had much to learn. They'd been hunting with the pack for only a few months.

Three other wolves were the male's offspring from the year before. Now almost twenty months of age, they were old enough to leave the pack and start families of their own. The last wolf was a brown-gray adult female. She was more than three years old but had never had pups.

Usually, only one female wolf in a pack breeds—the alpha female. But, a few months earlier, the female leader of this pack had inexplicably disappeared. The wolves howled frequently during the following nights, hoping to guide her home, but she never returned. Her absence was damaging to the pack, but such losses are common. The pack's remaining female ascended to the position of alpha.

Danger lurked in these woods. Loggers had clear-cut large blocks of trees near roads, creating open spaces that left wolves vulnerable to humans with guns. Crews of humans exploring for oil and gas had carved long, narrow swaths through the spruce and pine forest. Through them traveled the humans on snowmobiles who set traps for wolves. The big male knew to avoid even the slightest whiff of human scent. The younger animals weren't so wary. Like the alpha female, lesser pack members sometimes disappeared.

Just the week before, humans had caught three wolves from the pack in nooses of thin wire and hauled them away alive. The rest of the pack had last seen their brethren in the snares, their necks held taut. The pack milled around for nearly half an hour. The wolves knew their packmates were in trouble and probably would die. But they couldn't be sure.

Humans also had snared one of the pups from the pack several weeks earlier. He disappeared for two days, then returned with a black collar around his neck. No matter how hard he tried, he couldn't rid himself of the plastic band. In time, he ignored it, as did the other pack members.

Now the pack had full bellies. The previous day's hunt had been arduous but successful. Hunting had been difficult this winter, and the wolves had often gone hungry. Prey had been available, but the snowfall had been light and the weather moderate. The deer, elk, and moose that roamed the mountain foothills and muskeg bogs surrounding Petite Lake usually eluded the wolves. Fawns and calves that had been so easy to capture in the summer now were swifter, stronger, and much wiser.

Early the day before, the pack had started its patrol. The wolves traveled single file, taking turns breaking trail through the snow. At prominent spots, the alpha male and female marked their territory with urine—their way of posting "no trespassing" signs for other wolves. To ensure a regular supply of prey, they had to mark and defend a large territory.

The pack traveled at a steady pace, their back paws hitting the same spot recently vacated by their front, their narrow chests bringing their feet close together in pairs. Evolutionary forces had crafted an animal that could move efficiently through the snow for long distances.

Catching a scent at precisely the same moment, the wolves stopped in unison. Their tails stuck out stiffly behind them, and their noses plied the air. They all smelled moose—moose not far away. The young wolves gamboled about the adults, wagging their tails and whining excitedly. Then they were off, bounding through the snow in great leaps, their back paws now overreaching their front.

The pack slowed as the scent became stronger, dropping into single file again with the big black male now in the lead. Approaching cautiously from downwind, the wolves maneuvered close for a surprise attack. They became even more excited when they spotted their prey: a cow moose and a calf. Experience had taught them the calf was the prize they sought.

The wolves charged. The moose ran toward a thick patch of alders, the wolves snapping at their hocks. When they reached the shrubby trees, the big cow spun around and slashed at the wolves with her front hooves. She used her bulbous nose to nudge the calf into position behind her.

The big moose laid her ears back, pawed the ground, and

challenged the wolves to take her on. She warded off a few charges with her flying feet. Then the wolves, hungry but wary, retreated a short distance. A broken leg or even a single cracked tooth could bring them a lingering death. A few minutes later, the black male gave a few short barks, and the wolves attacked again. This time, the big male went as close to the flailing cow moose as he dared, while the female streaked behind and struck at the calf. The young moose, terrified at its momentary lack of protection, bolted from the alders. The cow quickly followed. All ten wolves pursued them.

The chase went on for nearly a mile. Nine times out of ten, the moose wins these contests. But this time, the pack caught up with the two moose in a large clearing. The calf, growing tired, trailed the cow by about ten yards. The alphas closed in on each side. The big male sank his teeth into the calf's haunch, tearing skin and ripping muscles. As the calf staggered, the alpha female rushed in and grabbed its nose, temporarily immobilizing the animal. The big male slashed again at the injured leg. Then the young wolves seized the opportunity to grab the beleaguered young moose. As the animal stumbled, the alpha female clamped her jaws around the calf's tender throat, killing it swiftly. The enraged cow charged back, driving the wolves away from her calf's lifeless body. She stood over it for nearly an hour before vanishing into the woods.

The wolves fed on the calf for two days. When dawn broke on the morning of January 10, only hide and a few bones remained. The pack had eaten even the skull and teeth. Sated, they settled in for a day of rest.

Meanwhile, twenty miles to the south, near the settlement of Hinton, Alberta, more than a dozen biologists and veterinarians from the United States and Canada were engaged in a whirlwind of activity aimed at fulfilling one of the most notable undertakings in the history of wildlife conservation.

The lives of the pack members would never be the same.

Shortly after dawn, while the wolves dozed, a Piper Super Cub lifted off the small runway at Hinton and headed north toward Petite

Lake. Local trappers recently had captured three male wolves there—the ones in the wire nooses—and had seen the tracks of a large pack. The pilot's headset was tuned to the frequency of the young wolf fitted with a black radio collar and released a few weeks earlier. The pilot soon picked up a soft beep that became stronger as Petite Lake loomed larger through his cockpit window. Then he saw dark outlines of animals on the snow: a wolf pack. He radioed the airport.

Within minutes, a Bell Jet Ranger helicopter was airborne, northbound from Hinton. The pilot occupied the right-hand seat, a biologist serving as spotter the left. A second biologist, who'd try to dart the wolves with a tranquilizer gun, sat in the right rear. The darter wore a jumpsuit the same color as the cardinal red chopper. A nylon harness made of seat belt webbing encircled his waist and upper legs like the harness of a parachute. The back of the contraption connected to a sturdy line affixed to the inside of the helicopter. This cord was his lifeline in case he leaned too far out. The pilot punched in numbers on his Global Positioning System scanner and made a beeline for Petite Lake, skimming about five hundred feet above the ground. The helicopter's receiver, also tuned to the radio-collared wolf pup, beeped steadily over the roar of the rotors.

Approaching the lake, the pilot shook his head. The terrain didn't look suitable for capturing wolves. Thick timber cloaked the rolling hills, offering few openings. Most of the clearcuts were studded with large snags—dead trees that make low-level flying extremely risky.

Then the spotter began pointing excitedly at a small clearing beside a clump of trees. He saw wolves there, at least half a dozen of them. The pilot veered away, found a clearing about a half a mile from there, and gently set the helicopter down. The spotter would wait on the ground. The flying would be fast and dangerous; there was no sense risking any more lives than necessary.

The crew removed the two doors on the aircraft's right side. The darter would have to lean far out of the aircraft, bracing one of his feet on the chopper's skid. He needed a big opening. He loaded his weapon: a Palmer capture gun, a device about the size and weight of a lightweight 20-gauge shotgun. It broke open at the breech and held a single dart loaded with Telazol, a drug that usually immobilizes a wolf within four to ten minutes.

Ready for action, the pilot and darter lifted off, gliding about fifty feet above the treetops back to where they'd caught sight of the wolves. The pilot would have to do some fancy maneuvering. The maximum distance for a shot would be fifty feet; less than twenty-five would be better. The tallest trees were sixty feet high. The strategy was to harry the wolves until one broke from the timber and ran out onto the frozen lake or across a meadow. Then the pilot would swoop down, follow the wolf, and let the darter fire his shot. Because the openings in the timber were so small, there would be time only to drop down, shoot, and pull up quickly.

The Piper Super Cub circled overhead, its pilot keeping an eye on the wolves and the helicopter. If the chopper crew darted a wolf, the airplane pilot would keep it in sight until the helicopter could set down and drop off the biologist to capture the drugged animal. The helicopter then would carry the wolves to a special compound near Hinton, where another team of biologists and veterinarians awaited them.

The helicopter crested a ridge, and the crew again spotted the wolves. The animals hadn't moved from where the spotter had first noticed them. But, as the helicopter neared, the wolves retreated to the safety of the dense trees, led by the black male with the silver throat.

The helicopter pilot zipped into position, hovering over the trees sheltering the animals. The wolves nervously paced the forest floor. Through the patch of dense timber, a long path led to a wide clearcut. If the wolves ran that way, the darter would stand a fighting chance.

Trees whipped in the wash of the helicopter's rotors, throwing up spirals of snow. One of the wolves darted out, heading down the path toward the clearcut. The pilot tipped the chopper forward and took off in pursuit. Timing was everything. If he began chasing the wolf too soon after it hit the clearcut, the wolf would turn around and run back into the trees. If the pilot waited too long, he risked running out of room on the opposite side of the clearing; the wolf would escape into the timber beyond.

When the wolf had almost reached the middle of the opening, the pilot made his move. He lurched forward and dropped within ten feet of the ground. The wolf looked over its shoulder, saw that it was in deep trouble, and ran for its life toward the distant trees. The hard snow in the meadow provided excellent footing.

The pilot's challenge was to match his speed and direction with the wolf's. He wanted to get within the ideal twenty-five-foot zone in which the darter could squeeze off a shot. If he got too close, the wolf would change direction and bolt. If he was too far away, the darter would miss.

The chopper zoomed in. The darter leaned out as far as he dared, then pulled the trigger. He could barely hear the report of the gun over the beating of the rotors. The dart hit the wolf square in the flank. The darter signaled thumbs-up as the pilot fought for altitude, just as the trees on the other side of the clearing closed in. The pilot radioed word of the successful shot to the spotter-plane pilot circling above.

After the helicopter landed, the crew followed the tracks and found the wolf a short distance away. They bound its legs, fitted a muzzle over its mouth, and carried it to the helicopter. Then it was back to the air to catch more wolves.

The other wolves had stayed in the thick cover. The pilot again hovered over the trees, unnerving the animals. They sought escape. One seemingly had found a path to freedom; perhaps others could, too. The big black male sprinted down the same path. The pilot buzzed down, dodged a snag, and positioned the darter for a shot. Again, the dart found its mark. The pilot radioed to the spotter plane to track this wolf closely; it was large and might not go down with a single dose of tranquilizer.

Sure enough, after ten minutes, the alpha male was still running for all he was worth. The airplane directed the helicopter to a good place to set down, from where the pilot and biologist trailed the big wolf on foot. Drag marks in the snow showed that the tranquilizer had taken some effect; the wolf was having trouble lifting his feet.

As the two men crossed a small hill, they spied the wolf about thirty yards ahead. They started running. Even when tranquilized, the animal could run almost as fast as his pursuers. When the men finally caught up to him, the wolf turned and snarled. The biologist and pilot knew they had an alpha; a subordinate wolf would have displayed doglike signs of submission. But the wobbly wolf was no match for two men. Using a "capture noose" on the end of a metal pole, the biologist held the animal still while the pilot jabbed the wolf with another dose of tranquilizer. Another wolf was in the bag— this one a mature alpha that might prove especially valuable.

One at a time, three more members of the pack attempted the ill-fated dash to freedom, including the brown-gray alpha female, who tried to hide in a slash pile in the middle of the clearcut. Each was captured. Only five members of the pack escaped.

The helicopter crew ferried five wolves of the Petite Lake pack to a maintenance building at Switzer Provincial Park, near Hinton. Biologists hoisted the lighter of the still-unconscious wolves over their shoulders and carried them into the building. They hauled the adult animals in on litters. The veterinarians quickly inspected the wolves for injuries and treated the dart wounds. Then the biologists examined the wolves closely to determine their age, sex, size, and reproductive ability. Everyone agreed that the large black wolf, which weighed ninety-eight pounds, was an alpha male. Judging from his tooth wear, he was four or five years old. His testicles were large and well-developed, indicating his status as a breeder.

The brown-gray female also received close inspection. Her well-developed nipples showed she was an adult, although the biologists guessed she'd never nursed. Her vulva was swollen, and flecks of blood dotted the hair near her vagina. This female, which also weighed ninety-eight pounds, would be ready to breed very soon.

The other three darted wolves were males weighing between

seventy and eighty pounds each. With testicles the size of raisins, they hadn't yet reached breeding age.

After the examination, biologists took blood samples; inserted ear tags (inside the ear so they wouldn't be visible); and took a small tissue sample from each wolf for genetic identification.

When the five Petite Lake wolves woke up, they found themselves inside individual twelve-foot-by-six-foot chain-link pens, reunited with the three other pack members trappers had snared earlier. The next day, the wolves were tranquilized, placed in small travel kennels, and loaded onto a USDA Forest Service transport plane headed for the United States.

Destined for Yellowstone National Park and central Idaho, nearly eight hundred miles south, the Petite Lake wolves were embarking on an extraordinary journey. Even more remarkable, though, was the seventy-year-long series of events that had made their journey possible.

HOW THE WEST WAS LOST

It was 1930. The wolf's howl had been silenced in Yellowstone National Park and most other locations in the contiguous United States. Few people shed any tears. Most celebrated. The *Denver Post's* headline over a news story about one of Montana's last wolves summarized the outlook of the day: "Ghostlike Marauder Terrorizes Ranchers Ten Years Despite Rewards—He Laughs at Airplanes, Guns, Traps, Poison and Continues Depredation."

By the turn of the century, westerners had invented a mythic wolf: an animal capable of decimating big game faster than a speeding bullet; a beast that could lay waste to entire herds of livestock in a single bound; a creature of monstrous cruelty and incredible cunning.

Many people have sharply criticized the wolf-killing ways of the West's early settlers. They fiercely denounce our ancestors' "pathological hatred" of the wolf. But it wasn't as simple as that.

Most Americans in the 1870s didn't understand biology. They had no concept of the interrelationships among members of natural systems. They based their view of nature almost exclusively on religious beliefs. Americans generally accepted what they read in the Bible: man was cast in the image of God, who placed him on Earth to have dominion over the rest of creation. To put their attitudes toward animals in perspective, it helps to realize that Charles Darwin's book *The Descent of Man* wasn't published until 1871—just about the time the western wolf wars began. That book revolutionized thinking about the relationship between man and nature, giving rise to the notion that all living things have value.

It's too easy to blame the excesses of earlier generations on hatred and mean-spiritedness alone. The more pertinent question? How has the world changed so much that the same country that sought to eradicate the wolf for most of the twentieth century now seeks to restore this animal at the beginning of the twenty-first? Why are attitudes different today from what they were at the turn of the century? We can best answer these questions by standing in the well-worn boots of the pioneers and seeing the new frontier through their wire-rimmed spectacles.

Before the colonization of North America, *Canis lupus* inhabited the entire continent except for the southeastern United States, home of the red wolf—*Canis rufus*. The gray wolf enjoyed the widest distribution of any land mammal. In fact, wolves are one of the most widely distributed species in the world, occurring across much of Europe and most of Asia.

In their 1944 classic, *The Wolves of North America*, Stanley Young and Edward Goldman identified twenty-three subspecies of wolves in North America. Two subspecies inhabited the Yellowstone region: *Canis lupus irremotus*, or the Rocky Mountain wolf, and *Canis lupus nubilis*, known as the Great Plains, or buffalo, wolf. These two subspecies were very similar in size and habits. Both wolves weighed about sixty to one hundred twenty-five pounds and were five to six feet long. Young and Goldman established these subspecies primarily on the basis of what they perceived as small differences in skull measurements.

Taxonomists (biologists who classify plants and animals into species, subspecies, and other categories) today recognize far fewer subspecies of wolves, as few as five in North America. They criticize the small sample size Young and Goldman examined to reach their conclusions. Taxonomists also point out that because wolves range so widely—the scientific literature reports movements of more than five hundred miles—the likelihood of purported subspecies' interbreeding, and thus sharing genes, is high. Modern taxonomists also have a tool not available fifty years ago: scientific tests that analyze the DNA of wolves. These tests reveal few differences in the genetic makeup of most North American wolves. One biologist has jokingly suggested a single classification: *Canis lupus irregardless.*

When Lewis and Clark led the Corps of Discovery through Montana in 1805 and 1806, wolves were abundant, especially on the rolling plains and sharp-sided coulees of eastern Montana. Their journals frequently report wolves' killing bison. Lewis called the wolves "shepherds of the buffalo" because he often found the species near each other. When members of the Corps killed a game animal for food, they had to guard it. Captain Clark noted, "All meat which is left out all night falls to the wolves which are in great numbers."

Early estimates of wolf numbers in the Yellowstone region exceeded thirty-five thousand animals. *Thirty-five thousand wolves.* Although this number may not be precise (the numbers come from harvest figures that sometimes included coyotes), it bears repeating because it makes our modern-day plans for wolf recovery seem so modest by comparison. The 1987 Rocky Mountain Wolf Recovery Plan—the government plan that sets restoration goals—calls for the establishment of at least three wolf populations of about one hundred animals each.

Fur trappers followed the trails that Lewis and Clark blazed, but until about 1830, they had little interest in wolves. Their quarry was the beaver. In fact, before 1850, people generally hunted wolves for sporting purposes, rarely for money. John James Audubon, the famous ornithologist, naturalist, and painter, reported during a trip up Montana's Missouri River in the 1830s: "The most interesting event of the day was the shooting of a wolf."

But during the 1850s and 1860s, the ever-fickle fur market shifted from beaver pelts to the hides of bison, deer, elk, and wolves. In 1853, the American Fur Trading Company shipped out three thousand wolf hides from outposts along the Yellowstone River, and the numbers continued to climb for the next several decades. By the mid-1860s, American Fur Trading Company outposts along the Missouri River shipped between five thousand and ten thousand wolf pelts a year.

Wolf pelts became so valuable between about 1860 and 1885 that demand for them spawned a peculiar new occupation: "wolfing." Because wolf pelts have economic value only in the winter, when the fur is thickest, wolfers labored seasonally. In the warm months, they worked in gold mines or on steamboats or tended livestock.

According to Montana historian Edward Curnow, "The wolfer's methods were simple and effective. He killed a buffalo every three or four miles and inserted strychnine into the entrails, tongue and flanks of the animal. The unsuspecting wolf ate the buffalo carcass and died near it." The results were devastatingly effective—at least early on, before wolves grew wary and some learned to avoid poison. Reports indicate that sometimes dozens of wolves lay dead near carcasses. The wolfers arranged their poison stations in a circular pattern to save travel time. They'd ride their circle every day or two to retrieve and skin dead animals. Killing wolves with poison was almost easy. Weather presented the only major difficulty. Wolfers couldn't skin frozen wolves properly, and warm weather could ruin the pelts. A trio of wolfers wound up with hundreds of frozen carcasses one winter and piled them in a mound overlooking the Missouri River in northeastern Montana. The mound briefly became a landmark for which a nearby town is named: Wolf Point. In his book *Forty Years on the Frontier*, early Montana pioneer and statesman Granville Stuart wrote that wolf pelts sold for two to three dollars apiece in the 1860s and 1870s; in a good winter, a wolfer could make two to three thousand dollars.

The wolfers and their poison posed the only real threat to wolves in the Yellowstone region before the 1870s. Neither cattlemen nor farmers had arrived in any numbers, so there was little organized persecution. Wolves also temporarily benefited from a parallel event in American wildlife history: the near-annihilation of the bison.

The 1870s were the decade when people slaughtered bison across the West, killing them most often for their hides but sometimes for only their tongues. The rate of decline was sharp—hundreds of thousands of animals a year. Discarded carcasses provided an incredible food source for wolves; they didn't even have the hard work of chewing through the thick hide to reach the meat. Buffalo hunters claimed that wolves used to come running at the sound of gunfire and stood waiting for them to finish skinning the bison they'd shot.

So, despite the pressure from wolfers, wolf numbers remained high in many areas. When wolves enjoy favorable conditions—their most critical need is good nutrition—they can breed at an earlier age, at $1^1/2$ instead of $2^1/2$. They also can produce more pups, as many as eight to ten instead of the usual four to six. Although we can't be sure, it's likely that wolf populations held their own when bison were in their steepest decline. But as bison populations dwindled and settlers began to migrate west, the wolves' prosperity proved short-lived.

Events of the 1880s and 1890s sealed the fate of wolves in the West and sowed seeds of hatred that would sprout for generations. The combination of two critical events—the near-eradication of the bison and other big-game animals and the boom of the livestock industry—produced a prejudice that remains alive and well today.

By the late 1870s, cattlemen had filled the region surrounding Yellowstone Park with livestock. Cattlemen from Texas, Nebraska, Kansas, and Colorado discovered that Montana's and Wyoming's prairie grasses maintained nutrition even during the winter and could carry livestock through all but the coldest weather and the deepest snow. Large cattle drives brought tens of thousands of livestock into

Montana and Wyoming during the early 1880s.

By 1884, only scattered herds of bison remained on Montana's and Wyoming's prairies. Although the slaughter of the bison is a well-known part of American wildlife history, most people don't realize that early settlers exploited *all* western game species. Miners, trappers, steamboat workers, and homesteaders all needed meat, and the outdoors was their larder. There were few laws limiting the take of game animals. Federal and state laws now prohibit "market hunting"—killing wildlife for sale to stores and restaurants—but the practice was common during that era.

Once the bison were gone, the settlers focused on elk, deer, moose, antelope, and bighorn sheep, exacting a terrible toll throughout the West. Even after the advent of modern wildlife conservation, it took almost half a century for big-game populations to rebound. Today, it's easy to take thriving big-game populations for granted. For instance, Montana's elk now number around ninety thousand, and there are more deer and antelope than people in Montana and Wyoming.

At the turn of the century, it was a different story. Populations of elk, deer, and antelope were at levels so low that, by modern standards, they'd qualify for endangered species listing. An old-timer reared on a farm near Montana's Bighorn River in the first decade of the twentieth century remembered that residents of the nearby town of Hardin traveled almost twenty miles by wagon in hopes of catching a glimpse of a deer reported near a neighboring farm; local people hadn't seen one for years.

Even more important was how rapidly people eradicated bison and replaced them with cattle. Granville Stuart wrote of Montana, "It would be impossible to make persons not present . . . realize the rapid change that took place on those ranges." In 1880, he said, you "could travel for miles without seeing so much as a trapper's bivouac. Thousands of buffalo darkened the rolling plains. There were deer, antelope, elk, wolves and coyotes on every hill and in every ravine and thicket." But by the fall of 1883, he reported, "there was not one buffalo remaining on the range, and the antelope, elk and deer were indeed scarce."

The decline of game animals did more than eliminate the wolves' prey base. As deer and elk numbers declined, sportsmen became increasingly militant about predator control. In 1886, *Forest and Stream* magazine—very influential at the time—published an article on wolves and panthers that captured the feeling of the day: "Montana is simply overrun with destructive wild animals at present," the author asserted. Largely in reaction to the decline of big-game populations in the West, Theodore Roosevelt organized the Boone and Crockett Club in 1887. It was the first wildlife conservation organization with a national focus.

Even conservationists like Roosevelt and William Hornaday had no use for the wolf. Hornaday wrote in his 1904 book, *The American Natural History*, "Of all the wild creatures of North America, none are more despicable than wolves. There is no depth of meanness, treachery or cruelty to which they do not cheerfully descend."

Wolves had few friends at the close of the nineteenth century. Stockmen and their allies despised them. Sportsmen, unwilling to share a vastly reduced prey base, supported wolf extermination. And no one had a good answer to the most commonly asked question about wolves: what good are they?

From a wolf's viewpoint, the arrival of vast herds of livestock in the early 1880s must have seemed a godsend. The cupboard had been bare. With their natural prey base depleted, wolves now had a choice: prey on livestock or die.

In the end, they did both. Hatred for wolves grew in direct proportion to the expansion of the western livestock industry. Although livestock producers probably embellished their reports for political reasons (they were lobbying state legislatures to create and increase bounties), ranchers clearly suffered heavy losses to wolves during the 1880s and 1890s. The Montana Bureau of Agriculture reported in 1894 that some Yellowstone County ranchers had lost more than half their calf crop to wolves and that the average loss rate was almost 25 percent. Many livestock reports from this era show a loss rate of 25 percent or higher. By contrast, livestock depredation in areas populated by wolves today is minimal, at worst—less than 1 percent. In Alberta, a province with more than four thousand wolves, losses attributed to them average less than one cow or calf a year for every thousand head of cattle in wolf habitat. In Minnesota, wolves claim less than one cow or calf each year for every eight thousand available to them. Such modest losses are the norm for areas with abundant wolf prey. It was a different story in the late nineteenth century, when wolves in the northern Rockies had little but livestock to eat.

Losses back then were so dramatic that many individual ranchers and some livestock associations hired men for the specific purpose of killing wolves. One group of ranchers near Fort Benton, Montana, paid wolfers five dollars (the equivalent of about fifty dollars today) for every wolf killed on its ranges. It's unlikely that ranchers would have paid such a high fee unless the risk of significant livestock losses had been real.

Wolf-eradication efforts were haphazard and disorganized until industry associations joined the fray. Like the Montana Stockgrowers Association, formed in 1884, many of the groups arose out of people's concern over wolf predation. The members of these organizations were among the earliest settlers. They had the most land, the most power, and the best political connections. They used their clout to persuade state and federal lawmakers to join the war on wolves.

On the state level, bounties that the territorial and state legislatures established became the main political avenue for wolf extermination. Once the bison were gone, most of the wolfers had packed up their poisons. Killing wolves had become increasingly difficult; it was no longer simply a matter of poisoning large carcasses almost certain to draw wolves. Shooting and trapping them required more time and skill. Ranchers understood that they needed to create greater incentives for people to kill wolves. The answer was bounties.

The first Montana bounty legislation, which the legislature

passed in 1883, awarded hunters one dollar for each wolf. Hunters had to show the hides to a probate judge or a justice of the peace. Then they could sell the pelts to fur buyers.

According to the Montana *Bounty Certificate Book*, during 1884—the first full year after the bounty act became law—bounty hunters presented 5,450 wolf pelts for payment. Wolf bounties continued in Montana until 1933—long after people had eliminated wolves in the state. Payments increased as wolves became more scarce. From the one dollar bounty in 1883, payment reached a high of fifteen dollars a wolf in 1911.

The politics of winning government funding then was exactly as it is today: the livestock industry had to convince a skeptical legislature that spending scarce resources for the benefit of one group was wise. The tactics were also familiar: to win support for bounty legislation, the livestock industry found it advantageous to magnify its losses and overstate the wolf's killing abilities.

During more than twenty years of fighting for bounties, ranchers embraced wolf-hating as part of the code of the West. Wolf-bashing came to rank with complaining about the weather and disparaging the federal government. Lore spread through weekly newspapers and gatherings of families and friends. Like the stories of western gunfighters, the legends grew bigger and wilder with each retelling. By the 1920s, they'd reached epic proportions. Consider how the *Dillon Examiner* eulogized the passing of the infamous Custer Wolf in 1921:

> The master criminal of the animal world, the Custer Wolf, has at last been killed. The death of the cruelest, the most sagacious, and most successful animal outlaw the range country has ever known was announced with a sigh of relief. . . . For nine years the Custer Wolf struck terror in the hearts of ranchers. Many credited the story that it was not merely a wolf, but a monstrosity of nature—half wolf and half mountain lion—possessing the cruelty of both and the craftiness of Satan himself.

There are dozens of other legends about Montana wolves; Snowdrift and the White Wolf of the Judith are among the most famous. Even today, it's impossible to talk with a group of ranchers without hearing that someone's grandfather or great-grandfather killed the last wolf in one locale or another. It remains in many corners a badge of honor to have done so.

The history of the destruction of wolves in Yellowstone Park took only a slightly different course from the events in the surrounding region.

When creating the park in 1872, Congress strictly prohibited the "wanton destruction of fish and game" within its boundaries. During the early years of its existence, however, the park was staffed by civilians who didn't tightly patrol it. It was a park only in name. Wolfers killed bison and elk and poisoned the carcasses with few consequences. Their actions significantly reduced wolf populations. According to the Yellowstone Park annual report for 1880, "The large ferocious gray or buffalo wolf, the sneaking, snarling coyote, and a species apparently between the two of a dark brown or black color, were once exceedingly numerous in all portions of the Park, but the value of their hides and their easy slaughter with strychnine-poisoned carcasses have nearly led to their extermination." The park's robust wolf population of the early 1870s was reduced to relatively few animals by 1880.

Lax wildlife protection in America's first park caught the attention of newspapers and magazines in the East. George Bird Grinnell, the editor of *Forest and Stream*, spearheaded the effort to protect Yellowstone Park's wildlife. Stories about poachers and market hunters slaughtering Yellowstone Park's elk and bison elicited a strong public response. Consequently, in 1886—under authorization given by Congress in 1883—the secretary of the interior appealed to the secretary of war to dispatch the First U.S. Cavalry to Yellowstone Park to protect its wildlife.

The troops arrived in August 1886. The military's by-the-book mentality provided an effective roadblock to poachers and market hunters eager to decimate Yellowstone Park's wildlife. Like most people in those days, however, the army was far more interested in protecting game animals than predators. Nevertheless, park records reveal few wolf killings in the park between 1886 and 1914.

Those same records show that park wolf sightings began to increase sharply around 1912. The superintendent's annual report for 1914 noted: "Gray wolves have made their appearance in the park in considerable numbers, having been seen traveling in packs of ten or less. While efforts have been made to kill them, thus far none have been taken inside of the park although a few have been killed just outside, along the northern border. . . . Efforts will be made to kill them."

By 1915, the wolves had already worn out their welcome. The superintendent's report characterized wolves as "a decided menace to the herds of elk, deer, mountain sheep and antelope."

Wolves might have survived in Yellowstone Park had not two federal agencies—the U.S. Biological Survey and the National Park Service—joined forces to destroy them. The Biological Survey, the forerunner of today's U.S. Fish and Wildlife Service, was the primary agent of predator destruction in the West. Congress created the Biological Survey in 1885 to promote research on wildlife and economics. In its formative years, under the direction of the great naturalist C. Hart Merriam, the agency distinguished itself as a protector of waterfowl. But around the turn of the century, under heavy pressure from the western livestock industry and its supporters, Congress redirected the agency's primary focus to predator control. The Biological Survey's major targets became wolves, coyotes, mountain lions, grizzly bears, and black bears across the western United States. It broke the western states down into districts and initiated a systematic program to eradicate predators.

In 1907, in cooperation with the Forest Service, the Biological Survey prepared a special report concerning "the enormous losses suffered by stockmen on western cattle ranges and the destruction of game on forest reserves, game reserves and national parks." The author of the report was Vernon Bailey, chief naturalist of the Biological Survey. As he explained in the February 1907 issue of *National Geographic* magazine, "The chief object of the report is to put into the hands of every hunter, trapper, forest ranger and ranchman directions for trapping, poisoning, and hunting wolves and finding the dens of the young." He claimed that each wolf cost stockmen about $1,000 a year.

But the real turning point came in 1914, when Congress appropriated special funds for the Biological Survey for "destroying wolves, prairie dogs, and other animals injurious to agriculture and animal husbandry." This funding put new muscle behind the agency's death-dealing programs.

The Biological Survey's aggressiveness in predator extermination had little respect for national park boundaries. In fact, Vernon Bailey himself spent considerable time in Yellowstone Park between 1914 and 1916, teaching army scouts how to find and destroy wolf dens. He warned that "constant care must be exercised to prevent their becoming reestablished in numbers to do serious damage to the game." Whereas the military's early predator-control efforts had been haphazard, Bailey got the army more organized and enthusiastic about wolf killing.

In 1916, Congress established the Park Service, and the administration of Yellowstone Park again became civilian rather than military. The Park Service mission seemed wolf-friendly enough. Congress had ordered the new agency to "conserve the scenery and the natural and historic objects and wild life therein, and to provide for the enjoyment of the same in such manner and by such means as will leave them unimpaired for the enjoyment of future generations." What the Park Service couldn't have known at the time was just how enthusiastic future generations would be about maintaining wolf populations.

The Park Service began managing Yellowstone Park during an extremely critical period for wolves. Their numbers were growing, and pressure to eliminate them was extremely high. In addition, big-game populations had rebounded in the park, and the surrounding states were counting on overflow of animals from the park to repopulate depleted areas nearby.

Once the fledgling Park Service took over in 1918, it succumbed to the same pressures that the military had. One of the first assignments of Yellowstone Park rangers became predator control. The Park Service finished what the military had started. Between 1914 and 1926, the government killed at least 136 wolves in the park. The most effective technique was the one Vernon Bailey favored: finding the wolves in their dens during the spring breeding season and destroying the whole family. Park records show that more than half the wolves killed during this period were pups.

Park Service rangers destroyed the last known den in Yellowstone Park in 1923, near Tower Falls. During the next three years, rangers or other government agents killed only a few wolves in the park. Park historians use a 1926 photo of two young wolves trapped at a bison carcass near Soda Butte, in the northeastern corner of the park, as the last firm evidence of wolves in Yellowstone Park. By 1930, wolf sightings in the park had decreased. Wolves now were more park visitors than denizens. People periodically reported wolf sightings over the next sixty years, including a spate of unconfirmed reports in the late 1960s and early 1970s, but no one has documented reproduction in Yellowstone Park since 1923.

Many deep philosophical and ethical treatises have examined why America exterminated its predators. We read discourses concerning the insidious impact of our northern European heritage and incisive psychological dissertations evaluating how centuries of folklore have created public hatred of wolves.

Yet the most obvious explanation for why people exterminated wolves still seems the best. It was self-interest, plain and simple, not malice or ignorance. If a pack of wolves today killed 25 percent of a rancher's livestock, we'd still destroy them. If wolves today threatened the existence of big-game populations, we probably wouldn't tolerate it; witness the struggles over wolf management in Alaska. The history

of the extermination of wolves in the West really isn't such a complicated story: There was an incredibly rapid shift from an abundance
of big-game animals and no livestock to virtually no big-game animals
and an abundance of livestock. Wolves switched their attention to
livestock and probably killed an enormous number of them. The
livestock industry—abetted by sportsmen concerned about the welfare
of big-game species—pressured state governments to offer bounties
and Congress to direct federal agencies to eliminate wolves. Witnessing
this animal's demise was a society that placed no value on the wolf.
End of story.

No, not quite.

THREE

CARRIERS OF THE TORCH

Les Pengelly, head of the University of Montana's wildlife biology program, burned with a bright flame. He was an average-sized man whose distinguishing feature was a completely bald head that seemed to bulge with ideas. He reminded me of Brainiac, the ultra-intelligent archenemy with the gleaming pate in *Superman* comic books. There was plenty that was funny about him. Quick-witted, he had a reputation in wildlife circles for owning "the fastest gums in the West." Proudly and pugnaciously honest, he displayed a Harry Truman quote in his office that read, "I never give them hell, I just tell them the truth and they think it's hell."

Exceptionally literate—he called himself a "cultural vagrant"—he was just as likely to quote Groucho Marx as he was Machiavelli. His nimble mind reveled in the nuances and ironies of people and their relationship to animals. Although he took his science seriously, he knew that social factors played a more important role in wildlife issues. He didn't begrudge the importance of politics in biology; he just wanted to make sure his students knew the score. I was one of those students. I was pursuing a master of science degree in environmental studies; my work combined wildlife biology and journalism.

The most popular course Pengelly taught at the university was "Biopolitics." He was fond of saying that wildlife biology was an art as well as a science; the art was in knowing what science to apply at the right time. He used this course to acquaint naive young students with the realities of fish and wildlife management. He brought extensive field experience to the task, having spent his formative years as a wildlife biologist lecturing often-skeptical miners and ranchers on the benefits of wildlife conservation.

Pengelly was deeply involved in both state and national wildlife issues. While I was his student (from 1974 to 1976), he served as president of The Wildlife Society, the nation's leading professional organization of wildlife biologists, and as a member of the Montana Fish and Game Commission, the agency that sets wildlife policy for Montana.

As I look back on those years, I find it amazing that Pengelly found time for an underinformed and naive graduate student like me.

Despite his prestigious positions, he never took himself too seriously. He'd say, "A person who's all wrapped up in himself makes a pretty small package." However, he took his professorial duties and his students very seriously. Because I showed interest in the leading wildlife issues of the day, he took me under his wing, spending many hours clarifying for me the intricacies of predator control, endangered species policy, and non-game wildlife protection.

He never tired of discussing the political machinations of natural resource luminaries. His favorite target for taunting was Frank Dunkle, Montana's former Fish and Game Department director. A couple of years earlier, Dunkle had unsuccessfully run for governor before starting a nonprofit group that worked for mining and timber interests. Pengelly viewed Dunkle as a political opportunist with no moral compass. Little did we know then that Dunkle would become one of the bigger obstacles to restoring Yellowstone Park's wolves.

But the issue that was nearest and dearest to Pengelly when I knew him—and the issue that won him a national reputation—was elk management in Yellowstone Park. He called this conflict "Malice in Wonderland." I was in school only a few months before I knew the story by heart.

A source of controversy since the turn of the century, Yellowstone Park's elk issue became a subject of a national debate during the 1960s when rangers began shooting large numbers of the animals in the park. Their goal was to trim the elk herds to bring them into better balance with available forage. But when park rangers slaughtered four thousand in one year, the public was outraged. Two major government-sponsored committees reviewed the situation in the early 1960s.

Their reports suggested that for national parks to give a "vignette of primitive America," park managers would need to let nature take its course. Yellowstone Park scientists already were thinking along these lines. They'd become skeptical of many of the assumptions upon which previous managers had based elk management in the park. In 1968—amid considerable controversy—Yellowstone Park adopted a new policy called "natural regulation." It was designed to reduce man's influence in the park. This policy halted the direct reduction of elk and relied on natural processes, including predation, to regulate elk populations. One glaring problem, of course, was that the most important predator of all—the wolf—was missing.

Pengelly and a bevy of other Park Service critics took great delight in spotlighting what they perceived as the scientific shortcomings of natural regulation. They called it a policy of convenience, a political response to an admittedly difficult problem. They raised the same questions then that some people ask today: does Yellowstone Park have too many elk, and do these elk overgraze the range and hurt other wildlife species? Pengelly and others argued that high elk numbers had reduced plant diversity in the park—particularly aspen and willows—thereby limiting the number of deer, songbirds, and beaver. Park Service officials contended that the range was healthy, not overgrazed, and that fire suppression, geology, and climate had caused changes in park vegetation.

I listened carefully to each installment of the Yellowstone Park elk story, always intrigued. The tale was intricate, filled with colorful characters locked in dissension. But one day I was brash enough to ask whether the debate was worth all the fuss. After all, elk in Montana were now as common as robins.

Luckily for me, Pengelly had great tolerance for both the unwashed and the unread. He rubbed his bald head; peered at me over his square, black glasses; and patiently explained how the defining event in American wildlife management history involved a single herd of deer—the Kaibab herd in Arizona. Their fate, he said, not only had influenced the management of deer and elk populations for generations but also had shaped thinking concerning the role of predators in natural systems.

The Kaibab Plateau, on the northern rim of the Grand Canyon, became a game preserve in 1906. At the time, national fear over declining deer and elk numbers had reached fever pitch. Spurred by President Theodore Roosevelt and early sportsmen's groups, federal agencies took action on the Kaibab. They called a moratorium on hunting and brought in the Biological Survey to control all predators: mountain lions, grizzly bears, coyotes, bobcats, and even the few remaining wolves. They also significantly reduced the livestock numbers on the range.

At first, the program seemed a great success; deer numbers surged. Unfortunately, they didn't stop rising. They increased until the deer had eaten almost all the available vegetation. Scientists agreed that the deer had become too plentiful, but the public's preservation sentiment ran so strong that agencies lacked the political will to kill the animals. By the mid-1920s, starvation sent the Kaibab deer herd into a steep decline that continued for the next decade.

The Kaibab deer story became a classic wildlife parable that appeared in wildlife texts for the next fifty years. The story evolved over time. At first, land managers offered it as proof that complete protection of game animals doesn't necessarily result in a healthy wildlife population. In later years, biologists like Aldo Leopold used the Kaibab example as stirring evidence of the dangers of overcontrolling predators. Later yet—in the 1970s—modern scientists completely discounted the Kaibab deer incident as offering any lessons at all. They argued that predator-prey systems are far more complicated than the simple cause-and-effect relationship suggested by the Kaibab example.

The Yellowstone Park elk issue has the same national significance as the story of the Kaibab deer, Pengelly said. He predicted that the elk controversy would become an equally important chapter in American wildlife history because it would provide guidance for managing large grazing animals as well as predators. The lessons we learned would apply to the world, not just the United States. Whether some African nation decided to save its elephants or lions might be a direct consequence of what the United States did with elk and their predators in Yellowstone Park.

Today, people have a much better understanding of the issues raised by the Kaibab deer and Yellowstone's elk. After all, even elementary school biology books unravel the complex relationships among predators, prey, and the other parts of the ecosystem. Terms like "food chains," "the web of life," and "survival of the fittest" are familiar to anyone who's ever browsed through a *National Geographic* magazine or tuned in to The Discovery Channel.

It's hard to believe that only fifty years ago, public understanding of such seemingly elementary concepts was extremely meager. But don't forget: it took scientists several centuries to convince the public that the world is round.

The biologists of the 1920s struggled to understand how natural systems worked. They perceived the intricate interaction of plants, animals, and the soil but hadn't yet developed the science to explain the connections. The best they could do was warn politicians of the dangers of discarding parts of natural systems people didn't understand yet.

By the mid-1920s, when wolves had been all but exterminated in Yellowstone Park, almost the only people complaining were a group of scientists from the American Society of Mammalogists. Many of the biologists in this professional society were affiliated with the nation's leading universities. Throughout the 1920s and 1930s, they repeatedly challenged the Biological Survey's policy of predator extermination. They reserved their fiercest objections for predator control in America's national parks.

Their opposition was right-minded but largely ineffectual, persistent but not persuasive. In 1931, Congress slapped down the opponents of predator control by passing the Animal Damage Control Act. This legislation increased the predator-killing budget and gave government agencies the broad authority to kill predators that persists to this day. Wildlife advocates did win a small battle. Use of poisons and steel traps in national parks was discontinued in 1931. All predator control in national parks ceased in 1935. But it was too late for Yellowstone Park; wolves were already gone.

Wolf supporters of the 1930s still hadn't succeeded in answering their opponents' most vexing question: what good is the wolf or any other predator?

In the 1930s and 1940s, wildlife biology turned from a philosophy into a science. Darwin's ideas built an intellectual framework for this metamorphosis. But science would have to prove that his concepts about evolution, including natural selection and survival of the fittest, were correct.

Paul Errington, a biologist, pioneered research on the effects of predators on their prey. He began his doctoral research at the University of Wisconsin in 1929, studying the impacts of gray foxes on bobwhite quail. He later moved to Iowa State University, where he continued his work on predators and their prey—studying mostly mink and muskrats—for the next three decades. In his classic work, *Of Predation and Life*, he emphasized how people frequently confuse the *fact* of predation with the *effect* of predation. In other words, just because one group of animals preys on another doesn't mean the predator controls that animal's population.

That was an important new perspective because, at almost the same time Errington published the results of his first study, Vernon Bailey of the Biological Survey completed a book with a very different outlook. In *The Animal Life of Yellowstone Park*, Bailey concluded, "It is therefore evident that wolves and game can not be successfully maintained on the same range."

Like Errington, two brothers, Olaus and Adolph Murie, made major scientific contributions to the body of knowledge that changed public and governmental thinking about predators. Their early work stemmed from the American Society of Mammalogists' continuing criticism of predator control around Yellowstone Park. Although the wolves were largely gone by 1930, rangers still killed coyotes within the park boundaries. Olaus Murie, the older of the brothers, studied coyotes in the Jackson Hole area, just south of the park, from 1927 to 1932. In *Food Habits of the Coyotes of Jackson Hole, Wyoming*, he reported what coyotes ate based on his examination of their stomach contents and scat. He found that rodents were the most significant part of their diet, elk a relatively small part.

Adolph Murie's work was more wide-ranging, as the title of his report *Ecology of the Coyote in the Yellowstone* suggests. He asked questions we'd expect from modern biologists: How do weather, food, and disease influence coyote survival? How do coyotes interact with various prey species?

His acute powers of observation paved the way for an important new approach to wildlife biology. It involved spending long periods of time in the field, drawing conclusions from observing animal behavior.

Adolph Murie spent 1940 and 1941 in Alaska, conducting America's first major study on wolf ecology. In his monograph *The Wolves of Mount McKinley*, he painted a picture of the wolf's complex social life. His words also evoked a new image of this beast of lore: "The strongest impression remaining with me after watching the wolves on numerous occasions was their friendliness."

Errington, the Muries, and like-minded biologists built the scientific foundation for wolf conservation during the 1930s and 1940s. But their vision of the connection between man and nature needed someone who could translate it into language that non-scientists could understand. Aldo Leopold was that spiritual leader.

Leopold was a Yale-educated forester who began his career in Arizona and New Mexico with the Forest Service in 1909—just about the time the Kaibab deer controversy began. He wrote most of his now-famous works when he was a professor of wildlife management at the University of Wisconsin. His earliest claim to fame was a 1933 book called *Game Management*, his vision of the art and science of the profession of wildlife management. Wildlife managers adopted the book as their professional bible and held up Leopold as the father of wildlife management in America.

Despite Leopold's many accomplishments and brilliant writing, most of his acquaintances never thought him a blinding intellect. On the contrary, they thought his greatest gift was his simplicity. A friend once observed that Leopold's thinking was "not that of an inspired genius, but that of any ordinary fellow trying to put two and two together." His defining characteristics were unbounded optimism and a common-sense approach to problem solving.

Leopold's intellectual evolution involving predators foreshadowed the progression the country as a whole would undergo on the way to restoring wolves to Yellowstone Park. He spent his early Forest Service days in the Southwest killing wolves, mountain lions, coyotes, and bears in their last strongholds as part of the government effort to increase deer populations. He considered this important work at the time. In a 1919 article, Leopold issued a shrill call for predator eradication:

> New Mexico is leading the West in the campaign for eradication of predatory animals. Our State Council of Defense has pooled its dollars with the U.S. Biological Survey in a mighty effort to rid the ranges of these pests. This effort has hung varmit [*sic*] scalps on the clothesline,

but it has just begun. It must keep on. This means dollars, not in dribbles, but in five figures—dollars without stint or limit. Quick work on varmits is the cheapest. Slow work, and bounties, merely remove the increase, and are sheer waste of money. The sportsmen and the stockmen—one-third of the population and one-half the wealth of New Mexico—demand the eradication of lions, wolves, coyotes and bobcats.

The Kaibab deer incident significantly affected Leopold. In addition, his acquaintance with many of the leading scientists of the day—including Errington and the Muries—changed his thinking about predators and predator management. He described the roots of his shift in the often-quoted essay "Thinking Like a Mountain," published as part of his posthumous *A Sand County Almanac* in 1949. Leopold harked back to an afternoon when he and his companions had shot a wolf after it had swum across a river in New Mexico:

> We reached the old wolf in time to watch a fierce green fire dying in her eyes. I realized then, and have known ever since, that there was something new to me in those eyes— something known only to her and the mountain. I was young then, and full of trigger-itch; I thought that be- cause fewer wolves meant more deer, that no wolves would mean hunter's paradise. But after seeing the green fire die, I sensed that neither the wolf nor the mountain agreed with such a view.

Leopold wrote those words in 1944, when he was becoming increasingly assertive about the need to restore a niche for wolves in the United States. That was also the year that Young and Goldman's classic book, *The Wolves of North America*, was published. Leopold clearly was no fan of Young and Goldman. Both had been longtime employees of the Biological Survey and aggressive advocates of preda- tor control and wolf extermination. In a review of the book published in the *Journal of Forestry*, Leopold wrote:

Viewed as conservation, *The Wolves of North America* is, to me, intensely disappointing. The next to last sentence in the book asserts: "There still remain, even in the United States, some areas of considerable size in which we feel that both the red and gray [wolves] may be allowed to continue their existence with little molestation." Yes, and so thinks every right-minded ecologist, but has the United States Fish and Wildlife Service no responsibility for implementing this thought before it completes its job of extirpation? Where are these areas? Probably every reasonable ecologist will agree that some of them should lie in the larger national parks and wilderness areas; for instance, the Yellowstone and its adjacent national forests. The Yellowstone wolves were extirpated in 1916 [actually, by the mid 1920s], and the area has been wolfless ever since. Why, in the necessary process of extirpating wolves from the livestock ranges of Wyoming and Montana, were not some of the uninjured animals used to restock Yellowstone?

Leopold's call for the return of wolves to Yellowstone Park was more conceptual than practical; it wasn't going to happen in the foreseeable future. Poisoned-bait stations designed to lure and kill coyotes still ringed the park. Public support for predators in general—let alone wolves in the park—was meager.

But Leopold, more clearly and ardently than anyone else, articulated the reasons why the public should care about predators. And he did so with poetry, as in his essay "The Round River." The mythical body of water, which Paul Bunyan discovered, flowed into itself in a never-ending circuit. Leopold used the river as a metaphor for the circular flow of natural systems. In doing so, he answered the question that no one else could: "The last word in ignorance is the man who says of an animal or plant: 'What good is it?' If the land mechanism as a whole is good, then every part is good, whether we understand it or not. If the biota, in the course of aeons, has built something we like but do not understand, then who but a fool would discard seemingly useless parts? To keep every cog and wheel is the first precaution of intelligent tinkering."

Leopold's writing stirred the winds of change, perhaps a slight breeze rather than a gale. But the change in the air was unmistakable.

FOUR

FROM VARMINTS TO ROCK STARS

Canada's Douglas Pimlott, a gentle but impassioned wolf biologist, recognized long before most people that science alone couldn't save the wolf. Leopold and others had explained why people *should* care about wolves. Pimlott found ways to *make* people care.

He understood that successful wolf conservation depended on public support, particularly from people who lived in the same areas as wolves. His 1967 article in *Defenders* magazine was one of the earliest calls for restoring wolves to Yellowstone Park, and he blazed a trail wildlife advocates would follow in achieving that goal.

In 1961, Pimlott posed what he called "the most important conservation question of our time" to fellow Canadians: "Will the wolf still exist when the twentieth century passes into history, or will man have exterminated it in a final demonstration of his conquest both of wilderness and of wild things that dare to compete, or that conflict with him?"

He feared that his country would repeat the mistake of the United States and seek to eliminate its wolves. And for good reason.

In the early 1960s, enormous hostility toward wolves prevailed in Canada. Government agents shot wolves from airplanes to decrease predation on big-game animals and, on the ground, poisoned wolves to protect livestock. Pimlott advocated protecting wolves in Canada's large parks and wildernesses. His integrity and honesty made him one of his country's conservation heroes. Pimlott's byword was "Candor but not confrontation, frankness but not rancor." Although he died in 1978, he remains the primary role model for Canadian researchers and wildlife agency employees.

Pimlott based his advocacy on science. After finishing his graduate work, he began studying wolves in Ontario's Algonquin Provincial Park, just over the border from Minnesota, in 1959. His wolf work provided rich material for articles and lectures he gave to audiences of park visitors. He also found a way to create opportunities for the public to have direct contact with wolves. He'd learned through his research that wolves would respond not only to tape-recorded wolf howls but also to human imitation of the haunting sounds. The imitation didn't even have to be especially good. By howling, Pimlott had been able to find and count wolves.

Part of his evening lectures soon included piling people into cars—the caravans sometimes exceeded 150 vehicles—and motoring down lonely, moonlit roads to remote locations. Once they'd reached their destination, the group would howl, hoping to inspire a wolf to respond. Their success delighted them.

"Almost inevitably the silence that follows the end of the howling of the pack is suddenly broken by an intense babble of the voices of the people all talking together, excitedly sharing the thrill of a superb wilderness experience," Pimlott wrote. "Almost inevitably, too, disinterest fades and people begin to understand why man should always be prepared to share his environment with creatures of nature."

Wolf support in Canada began to build.

Around the time Pimlott started his wolf research in Algonquin Park, Durward Allen of Purdue University, one of the United States' foremost wildlife biologists, sought students for an ambitious new wolf research project. The location would be Michigan's Isle Royale National Park. The unusually cold winter of 1948-1949 had created a bridge of ice linking the Ontario mainland with the forty-five-mile-long island in northern Lake Superior. Wolves crossed the ice and made themselves at home on the island, taking advantage of its substantial moose population. Isle Royale's isolation and consequent freedom from outside influences made it uniquely suited to studying interactions between wolves and their prey.

Because Allen wanted only the best students, he cast a wide net. A friend of his, a Cornell University professor, arranged for him to meet a promising but decidedly unworldly young student named L. David Mech. During the meeting, Allen spun a grand tale of the "mystical" Isle Royale and the unique research opportunities it presented.

Mech was impressed with Allen and his important work. But he already planned to undertake graduate work studying coyotes in the Adirondack Mountains of New York. He was puzzled that the famous biologist had taken time to describe this fantastic research project to him. "I'd never dreamed of going outside of New York State," Mech said to me years later. "After he told me all about Isle Royale, I told him it sounded like a great project and wished him the best of luck. Then he asked me if I'd like to do it. Holy cow! That's how it struck me."

Mech spent three years studying the wolves of Isle Royale and earning his doctorate from Purdue. A wolf star was born. *National Geographic* featured him and Allen in a 1963 story on wolves, the magazine's first on the subject in twenty years. Already well on his way to becoming the nation's leading wolf authority, Mech next wrote *The Wolf: The Ecology and Behavior of an Endangered Species* in 1970. It's the most comprehensive book of wolf science published to date.

The book is more than a scientific tome. At the end, echoing the voice of his colleague Pimlott, Mech wrote: "If the wolf is to survive, the wolf haters must be outnumbered. They must be outshouted, outfinanced, outvoted. Their narrow and biased attitude must be outweighed by an attitude based on understanding of natural processes. Finally their hate must be outdone by a love for the whole of nature, for the unspoiled wilderness, and for the wolf as a beautiful, interesting and integral part of both."

Like Pimlott, Mech understood that science alone couldn't save the wolf.

Scientists were, however, continuing to influence significantly how people viewed wolves. Films and books in the 1960s and 1970s no longer portrayed wolves as vicious killing machines but as animals that help maintain nature's balance.

Decades ago, Adolph Murie educated his fellow scientists with his monograph *The Wolves of Mount McKinley.* But it was Canadian writer Farley Mowat's 1963 book, *Never Cry Wolf,* that first informed the broad public about lupine habits and touched off America's love affair with wolves.

Murie's scientific report and Mowat's book are astonishingly similar, including the climactic scene in which the author enters a wolf's den. Although Mowat insisted that the experiences were his own, much of his book seems borrowed. Because he gave other researchers no credit, the book received brutal reviews from scientists. One of them was Pimlott.

Pimlott described the book as a blend of "fancy, fantasy and the published data of other workers." While acknowledging Mowat's skillful and sympathetic portrayal of wolves, he concluded, "I would delight in much of *Never Cry Wolf* if it had been presented as what it really is—fiction based on fact. The presentation of it as nonfiction, however, is at least deplorable." Nonetheless, this book did more to arouse the public's interest in and concern for wolves than had all the previous scientific works combined.

As wolf research expanded, wolf science became a staple of wildlife television programs like National Geographic Society specials, the Public Broadcasting Service's *Nature* series, and Mutual of Omaha's *Wild Kingdom.*

With all the good publicity wolves were now getting, it was no wonder that the public's attitude toward wolf conservation changed. Today, most Americans believe that wolves deserve a place in our world, although outposts of frontier resistance remain. And the media depict wolves in a way totally unlike that at the turn of the century.

Just look around. The changed climate for wolves is visible everywhere. Wolf designs adorn our T-shirts, slippers, coffee mugs, beer cartons, even our pajamas. Cuddly stuffed-toy wolves take their place on store shelves alongside teddy bears. In 1984, the rock band Los Lobos (Spanish for "The Wolves") released the hit song and album "How Will the Wolf Survive?" In the 1980s and early 1990s, the films *Never Cry Wolf, White Fang,* and *White Wolf* further popularized wolves. The 1990 movie of the year, *Dances with Wolves,* portrays the wolf as friendly, inquisitive, a tragic hero. According to the Humane Society of the United States, as many as three hundred thousand people in the country now own wolf-dog hybrids.

The cultural changes of the 1960s and 1970s brought important environmental changes as well. Two landmark conservation events of the 1970s cracked open the door to Yellowstone Park wolf restoration.

The first critical event, the banning of predator poisons, happened unexpectedly. Eagle poisonings in Wyoming during the 1960s had fueled strenuous protests against the federal predator control program. Still, most conservationists' jaws dropped in early 1972 when President Nixon announced in his "State of the Union" address an end to the use of predator poisons on public lands. He also promised to seek legislation to stop predator poisoning on private lands. Many people saw Nixon's action as a shrewd reelection strategy to offset his unpopularity for advocating the Alaska pipeline, but he kept his promise. For the first time in nearly a century, the public lands of the West—including those immediately adjacent to Yellowstone Park—were free of predator poisons. This single action did more than anything else to make the West once again habitable for wolves and many other predators.

The second landmark event was Congress's enactment of the Endangered Species Act. Although controversial today, the act passed in 1973 with only a handful of dissenting votes. Because the act mandated protecting listed species, including the wolf where it survived in the lower forty-eight states, conservationists finally found themselves in the driver's seat. Until then, they'd had to prove that helping wildlife wouldn't hurt the economy or stop development. Now representatives of the timber, mining, livestock, and other industries had to show that their actions wouldn't jeopardize endangered or threatened species.

For the first time in modern history, a nation had decided that wildlife—at least, certain species—was more important than traditional notions of progress and development. The new law helped set the stage for serious consideration of restoring wolves to Yellowstone Park.

One of the most baffling chapters in the saga of Yellowstone Park wolf restoration began to unfold in 1967. The number of wolf sightings in the park skyrocketed. Wolf reports there certainly were nothing new. Even after rangers purportedly had killed the last wolves in the park in 1926, visitors continued to report sightings. Between 1926 and 1966, visitors and park employees reported an average of more than twenty sightings each decade, mostly of single animals. Park officials found more than half of the reports credible enough to classify as "probable." None was confirmed.

But over a ten-year period starting in 1967, people filed more than four hundred reports, and park officials deemed more than a quarter of them probable. Many people reported seeing a group of five animals.

Many critics, including Les Pengelly, attributed the increased sightings to wishful thinking on the part of the Park Service. They contended that the agency saw a wolf behind every bush in order to sell the public on its new natural-regulation policy; it behooved the Park Service to give the impression that wolves, not rangers, were diminishing the elk herd.

The Park Service changed its techniques for tabulating wolf sightings in 1968 and believed that the new system contributed significantly to increased records of sightings. But even this change doesn't seem to explain the noticeable spike in reported wolf sightings.

It's equally unlikely that the tendency to mistake coyotes for wolves accounted for the surge in wolf reports in Yellowstone Park. The error is easy for lay people to make; although coyotes are less than half the size of wolves, large coyotes with thick winter coats can bear a strong resemblance to wolves. But qualified biologists—people who had spent time in Alaska or Canada and could readily distinguish between wolves and coyotes—had reported some of the sightings.

A wildlife detective might offer three theories to explain the mystery: a small wolf population had somehow persisted in Yellowstone Park; a few wolves from Canada had made it down to the park; or someone had released captive wolves there.

The first two theories don't stand up to scrutiny. Given Yellowstone Park's open vistas, its high visitor use, and the intensive grizzly bear and elk research going on in the park at the time, it's hard to believe that no one would have detected the presence of an animal that travels in packs, howls frequently, and leaves tracks and bloody kills in the snow. When wolf packs returned to Montana's Glacier National Park in the mid-1980s, people noticed them almost immediately.

Nor was it likely that several Canadian wolves had populated Yellowstone Park. In the late 1960s, the nearest wolf population was almost four hundred miles away, in southern Canada. Although scientists have reported wolf movements of more than five hundred miles, such forays are rare. In addition, Canadian wolves had been hit hard by control programs during the 1960s, so pressure for the wolves to disperse in search of an adequate food supply was low. Besides, to migrate to the park, the animals would have had to evade leg-hold traps; poisoned-bait stations; and rifle-toting, wolf-hating ranchers. Finally, even if Canadian wolves had migrated to Yellowstone Park, surely people occasionally would have reported seeing the animals as they passed through Montana. But records of the Montana Department of Fish and Game (now the Department of Fish, Wildlife and Parks) show no major increase in wolf activity during this period.

This leaves only the possibility that someone released captive wolves in Yellowstone Park in the 1960s. The Park Service's arch-critic, Montana writer Alston Chase, accused the Park Service of doing just that. But his 1986 book, *Playing God in Yellowstone*, offered no proof, only assertions. The clinching scene of his chapter on wolves is a Watergate-style conversation in which an unnamed park ranger tells Chase that the Yellowstone Park superintendent had revealed to him the park's dirty little secret: wolves had been a Park Service plant.

The Park Service vehemently denies any role in a clandestine planting of wolves, and such a conspiracy seems highly improbable. It's far more likely that private individuals—either wolf owners disposing of unwanted pets or wolf advocates disgruntled over governmental inaction—released some wolves.

Dave Mech, who by now had firmly established himself as the nation's leading wolf expert, took the rumors seriously enough to mention them in a 1973 publication on the status of wolves in the United States. "There are persistent rumors that the Yellowstone wolves are imported from Canada and released," he wrote.

Whatever the explanation for the earlier wolf sightings, reports of wolves in Yellowstone Park diminished during 1971 and shifted to national forest areas in Wyoming and Montana. If someone had planted wolves in the park, the animals apparently didn't stay.

The confusion over whether wolves actually had returned to Yellowstone Park caused considerable damage to wolf restoration efforts. Park Service officials had done such an exceptional job of convincing the public that the park might have wolves that now many people questioned whether reintroduction was necessary. This debate foreshadowed later controversies over reintroduction versus allowing wolves to return on their own.

Then, in 1972, Assistant Secretary of the Interior Nathaniel P. Reed called a major meeting in Yellowstone Park to discuss wolf restoration. He was all for the project and wanted to get the ball rolling. Among the people attending were Mech; Maurice Hornocker, the nation's foremost mountain lion expert; Amos Eno, Reed's assistant; and several members of the park staff.

What resulted from this meeting was a new Yellowstone Park wolf strategy that drove events for the next several years. According to the plan, a biologist would thoroughly survey the park to find out, once and for all, whether wolves were present. If he found no breeding animals, the agency would begin planning restoration.

In 1974, the Park Service hired John Weaver to conduct the survey. He spent his evenings poring over historical records and evaluating the authenticity of decades of wolf sightings. By day, he hiked, skied, and flew over the park, looking for wolf tracks and scat, listening for howls, always hoping to catch a glimpse of the elusive *Canis lupus*. He used time-lapse photography to try to capture on film wolves feeding on carcasses of road-killed elk and bison. He used Pimlott's technique of playing tape-recorded howls in hopes of at least hearing a wolf. Once, he thought he heard a wolf respond to his tape. But he never turned up a wolf.

Twelve months of intensive field work led Weaver to a firm conclusion: no viable wolf population existed in Yellowstone Park. Nor could he find evidence of any consistent reproductive activity in the fifty years since wolf control in the park had ceased. Still, even he didn't completely dismiss the conspiracy theory advanced by Alston Chase. "The possibility of a surreptitious release of captive wolves by private individuals cannot be totally discounted," he asserted in his report. But whatever wolves might have been released there now apparently were gone.

His 1978 *Wolves of Yellowstone* report ended with a succinct proposal: "I recommend restoring this native predator by introducing wolves to Yellowstone."

Although public awareness and acceptance of wolves had grown tremendously, conservationists still would have to fight an uphill battle before restoration would become a reality. Back then, of course, people had no idea just how long and bitter a struggle that would be. Maybe it's just as well they didn't.

FIVE

RETURN OF A LEGEND

The Bearpaw Wolf drifted down from the north, confounding skilled trappers and terrorizing ranchers for nearly twelve months. He slaughtered the choicest livestock, then disappeared without a trace. The four-legged Houdini loped past every kind of danger, sniffing out from hundreds of yards away every feeble attempt to ensnare him. The most carefully hidden traps were as visible to him as a mirror in the sun; he scornfully lifted his leg to them, treating them as a dog would a fireplug. Or so the stories went.

This wasn't 1915. It was late 1980, and one of the first wolves in nearly fifty years had returned to north-central Montana. Between December 1980 and December 1981, his legend grew as his alleged trail of livestock destruction widened. Wildlife managers never verified any of the losses. But by the time the wolf's reign of terror ended, local ranchers and employees of Animal Damage Control (a division of the Fish and Wildlife Service, later absorbed by the Department of Agriculture) credited him with killing eleven yearling cattle, one cow, twenty-five calves, two colts, sixteen lambs, nine ewes, one ram, and even someone's Thanksgiving turkey.

He also nearly killed fledgling wolf recovery efforts. The Bearpaw Wolf caught the U.S. Fish and Wildlife Service by surprise. Although people had reported wolf sightings in the Glacier Park area, no one considered the livestock-saturated plains of central Montana potential wolf country. The agency had no policy for dealing with livestock-killing wolves and no one on staff adept at capturing them.

At first, the Fish and Wildlife Service didn't want to kill the Bearpaw Wolf. After all, he was an extraordinarily rare find. Some biologists were as excited as if they'd discovered the long-lost black-footed ferret. So, the agency instead told Animal Damage Control to capture the animal, hoping to release him in the Glacier Park area.

That hope faded quickly. Animal Damage Control, which had a knack for killing animals, showed little aptitude for taking them alive. As the months wore on, livestock depredation reports mushroomed; every animal that died in central Montana supposedly had fallen victim to the infamous Bearpaw Wolf. Wolf hysteria—dormant for many years—sprang back to life with a vengeance.

The Fish and Wildlife Service didn't know what to do. It wanted to save the wolf but felt pressure from all sides to kill him. Relocating an animal blamed for killing over $18,000 worth of livestock no longer seemed tenable. It would have been easier to spring mass-murderer Charles Manson from prison.

The only solution was to destroy the Bearpaw Wolf, but agency employees feared that killing the animal would be illegal. The Endangered Species Act permits killing endangered species only under certain circumstances, and the Fish and Wildlife Service didn't think this one qualified.

The agency took another approach. Jim Hoover, Animal Damage Control district supervisor in central Montana, wrote about it in an internal memo never intended for public distribution. His memo describes how the Fish and Wildlife Service's endangered species employees and law enforcement agents urged Animal Damage Control to "kill the animal and be quiet." He claimed that people from the

Fish and Wildlife Service's Washington, D.C., office had suggested that he "kill the animal and claim it died from being over-tranquilized."

He carried out neither of those two plans. Animal Damage Control already suffered a bad enough reputation for its excessive animal killing. Hoover and his immediate superiors had no intention of adding to it by doing another agency's dirty work. The division said no, thank you.

The Fish and Wildlife Service took still another tack. Despite a lack of supporting evidence, it declared that the Bearpaw Wolf was actually a wolf-dog cross, an animal with no legal protection. The Bearpaw Wolf became the Bearpaw Dog. Having covered its backside, the Fish and Wildlife Service officially ordered Animal Damage Control to kill the animal.

Animal Damage Control had fumbled its live-capture assignment. It had balked at covering up an intentional killing by calling it an accident. But it snapped to attention once the Fish and Wildlife Service issued the kill order. The very next day, December 30, 1981, an Animal Damage Control agent flying in a small airplane found the tracks of the Bearpaw Wolf, followed them for fifteen miles, and blasted him into oblivion with a heavy dose of double-ought buckshot from a 12-gauge shotgun.

Less than a month later, the Montana Department of Fish, Wildlife and Parks' research lab in Bozeman verified what the agencies already knew: the Bearpaw Wolf was, indeed, a wolf, not a hybrid. His mounted carcass stood for many years in a glass case at the agency's headquarters, in Helena.

The Fish and Wildlife Service and Animal Damage Control traded accusations in the wake of the incident. In a letter to his supervisor, Hoover complained: "I believe the lack of responsibility, or the lack of authority to take responsibility, by these people who are supposedly in charge of the wolf's future should preclude any future consideration of the reintroduction of wolves." Animal Damage Control and its close ally, the livestock industry, made it clear that the Fish and Wildlife Service could expect tremendous opposition from them if it didn't develop a coherent plan for controlling wolves that kill cattle.

Around the time the Bearpaw Wolf was terrorizing central Montana, the Northern Rocky Mountain Wolf Recovery Team was finishing the first plan for restoring wolves in the region. The Fish and Wildlife Service had assembled the group in 1975 to carry out the mandate—outlined in the Endangered Species Act—to prepare plans for restoring the species. The recovery team, one of the first in the western United States, included biologists from state and federal agencies; a representative of the National Audubon Society; and Bob Ream, a University of Montana forestry professor. The only member experienced with wolves, Ream had studied these creatures with Dave Mech in Minnesota. For the others, membership on the team meant on-the-job training.

The recovery plan the team produced was a study in superficiality. Completed in 1980, it didn't tackle the tough questions: Where should agencies restore wolves? What should the goals for wolf populations be? How will the government manage wolves that attack livestock? The plan also didn't mention reintroducing wolves to Yellowstone Park. To conservationists hungry for progress in wolf restoration, the document came as a bitter disappointment.

In the vaguest of allusions to Yellowstone Park, the tepid plan presented a timetable for restoring wolves by 1987 to "areas where self-sustaining populations do not now exist." Only the most knowledgeable and optimistic people could infer from the plan any thoughts of reintroducing wolves to Yellowstone Park; this required a lot of reading between the lines.

But 1987 seemed a millennium away. And, given its lack of leadership and knowledge, the team wasn't likely to improve the recovery plan. The Endangered Species Act had created important new responsibilities for federal agencies. But it was easy for government employees to spend more time analyzing than actually carrying out the law.

While the recovery team fiddled around, the wolves took matters into their own paws: they started walking to Montana from Canada.

In the 1970s, people had reported dozens of wolf sightings just north of Glacier Park, in British Columbia. The accounts seemed credible enough that in 1973, the recovery team's wolf expert, Bob Ream, created a University of Montana research group called the Wolf Ecology Project. Members of the project investigated sightings and led wolf-education programs in northwestern Montana. Ream and his students played a critical role in promoting acceptance of wolves in that part of the state. At first, the Wolf Ecology Project garnered little government support, financial or otherwise.

In 1979, Ream's researchers captured their first wolf. They trapped an adult female along the Flathead River, just eight miles north of the Canadian border. They quickly released her after fitting her with a collar containing a tiny radio transmitter. Team members could then track the movements of the wolf by tuning a receiver to her specific frequency. They soon discovered that the wolf ranged on both sides of the border. By 1982, a wolf they believed to be the same animal had found a mate and produced a litter of eight pups north of the border, near Glacier Park. Because of their propensity for disappearing and reappearing, the family became known as the Magic Pack. Their advent marked the first continuous wolf activity in the western United States in more than half a century. This was a red-letter event.

During this period, wolf sightings also picked up in central Idaho. In June 1978, an Idaho Department of Fish and Game biologist snapped a photo of a black wolf in the Clearwater National Forest. Then, just a few months later, someone shot and killed a gray-colored wolf in the Boise National Forest, about two hundred miles farther south. These sightings underscored the need for the wolf recovery team to improve its plan. As the blueprint for managing wolves, it absolutely had to spell out in plain language exactly where wolves were welcome, the size of desirable wolf populations, and how to deal with wolves when they killed livestock. Wolves were busy reclaiming long-lost habitat, plan or no plan.

Wolf restoration was exceedingly controversial, and the recovery team seemed incapable of action. Its members froze like deer in the headlights of an oncoming truck. Far from producing a workable and straightforward plan for releasing wolves into Yellowstone Park, they couldn't deal even with the reality of wolves' recolonizing Montana and Idaho.

That was the situation Wayne Brewster waded into in 1979 when he hired on as the Fish and Wildlife Service supervisor of the endangered species program for Montana and Wyoming. When he moved into the agency's office in Billings, Montana, he brought with him the education of a wildlife biologist and discipline of a soldier. After earning a wildlife degree, he'd served for three years as an artillery officer in the army, including a combat stint in Vietnam. His forte was organizing and planning; he reveled in tactics and strategy.

He quickly deduced that the wolf recovery team needed a strong leader. His first step was to try to find one the livestock industry respected but didn't own. He needed someone who could go toe-to-toe with the cowboys and survive.

Bart O'Gara, leader of the Montana Cooperative Wildlife Research Unit, fit the bill. He became the recovery team leader in early 1981. This short, bald man radiates power and practicality. Like Brewster, he had been in the military before becoming a wildlife biologist and has a can-do attitude. Much of his research had involved predators; he'd recently finished studying golden eagle predation on lambs in southwestern Montana and coyote predation on sheep in Montana's Bitterroot Valley. Because his studies revealed the sometimes serious impacts of predators on livestock, the livestock industry viewed him as a straight shooter. The metaphor is apt; O'Gara has no compunction about pulling the trigger on problem animals. In fact, he has little trouble plugging creatures of any kind. His accomplishments as a sport hunter are legendary. He has more animal mounts in his home than do most museums.

Brewster also knew that every successful team needs members

with a variety of skills. He assembled a group of scientists and agency representatives knowledgeable about both wolves and governmental procedures. Perhaps the most important addition to the recovery team was John Weaver, the Wyoming biologist who'd surveyed Yellowstone Park for wolves in the mid-1970s. He now worked for the Forest Service as a wildlife biologist in the Bridger-Teton National Forest.

Weaver brought passion and energy to the team. His acquaintance with pioneer conservationist Adolph Murie and Olaus Murie's widow, Mardy, had stoked in him a fervor for conservation. Both Muries lived in Jackson, Wyoming, and Weaver frequently talked with them about wolves, coyotes, and the Muries' Alaskan adventures. "It was impossible not to be inspired by knowing people like the Muries," Weaver told me. "They not only were exceptional field biologists, but they were activists as well—people who devoted their entire lives to wildlife conservation."

Joe Helle, one of the most influential sheep ranchers in southwestern Montana, brought something quite different to recovery team meetings: a hatred for predators. He knew all about animals with teeth and claws; his ranch was where O'Gara had documented high lamb losses to golden eagles. Helle had been leaning on the secretary of the interior for several years to issue permits to kill eagles. His sheep range, in the Gravelly Mountains, also contained large populations of coyotes and black bears. These animals enjoyed the taste of lamb chops as much as the next predator.

Helle chaired the Montana Wool Growers Association's Predator Committee and was an active member of the National Wool Growers Association. He seemed to have a direct phone line to most western members of Congress. He was college-educated and could be polite— even charming—when necessary. If there was one thing that made his blood boil, it was talk about wolf restoration. Helle found it inconceivable that anyone would knowingly unleash such a plague on humankind; to him, restoring wolves was akin to reestablishing smallpox. During most recovery team meetings, his thick neck burned red at the thought.

"The time of the wolf is over," he'd thunder. "The ecological niche for wolf populations does not exist anymore because the vast herds of wild ungulates formerly providing the prey base for wolves have been replaced by domestic livestock. The wolf is like the buffalo and the dinosaur; his time has come and gone."

I often thought Helle might change his mind if he'd spend a weekend with me in Yellowstone Park around mid-February—when twenty thousand elk and up to eight hundred bison crowd the winter range in the northern part of the park.

Helle wasn't a recovery team member, nor was I, although we both attended almost every recovery team meeting. I'd begun working for Defenders of Wildlife in 1978. The issue of wolf restoration provided a perfect focus for two of Defenders' major conservation concerns: large predators and endangered species. Helle and I quickly became adversaries. Proposing a jaunt to Yellowstone Park to show him a prey base other than livestock was out of the question.

Timm Kaminski and Renée Askins also regularly attended recovery team meetings and supplied large doses of youthful enthusiasm. Kaminski, who'd recently received a wildlife biology degree from the University of Wyoming, had done volunteer work with Mech in Minnesota. That experience, coupled with his willingness to help the recovery team in any way possible, made him an important asset. Fresh out of Michigan's Kalamazoo College, Askins had moved to Wyoming to do volunteer work for John Weaver. She'd become enamored of wolves while studying a captive pack in Indiana as part of a senior-year project. She could spout poetry or quote *Of Wolves and Men* author Barry Lopez on demand; when she did, it drove Helle off the deep end. Recognizing Askins's excellent media skills, Weaver put her to work developing a slide show that would explain the recovery plan to the public. In time, Kaminski and Askins became important players in restoring wolves to Yellowstone Park.

Bolstered by O'Gara's leadership and Weaver's energy, the new recovery team made progress. The group started by defining places where state and federal agencies could restore wolves. The team agreed that recovery areas must be large, relatively free of livestock, and predominantly public land. Three areas emerged: the region including Glacier Park and the Bob Marshall Wilderness Area, in northwestern Montana; the Frank Church-River of No Return and Selway-Bitterroot Wildernesses, in central Idaho; and the Yellowstone Park area.

Next, the team tried to define how federal agencies should manage those three areas to promote wolf recovery. Past controversy over grizzly bear management in some of the same areas made this a sensitive assignment. Nevertheless, Weaver took the lead, drafting a set of wolf management guidelines for review by recovery team members and people who often attended their meetings. Helle and I received our copies in May 1982.

Helle didn't waste his time reviewing the document. Instead, he did the western equivalent of standing up in a crowded theater and yelling, "Fire!" He ran to his copy machine and cried, "Wolf!" He distributed copies of the draft plan to the congressional delegations and governors of Montana, Idaho, and Wyoming, along with his alarmist interpretation of it. According to him, federal agencies planned to curb logging, mining, and grazing on public land—all on behalf of the wolf. For the first time, western politicians came down hard on wolf recovery, besieging O'Gara with phone calls and burying him with a blizzard of angry letters. Idaho Senator Steve Symms went so far as to file a Freedom of Information Act request for documents belonging to the recovery team. He wanted to know whether the group was engaged in wolf restoration activity, and he didn't trust the members to come clean without being forced to do so. Symms's message was clear: this is war.

Meanwhile, Representative Larry Craig of Idaho had cooked up another scheme sure to make wolf proponents squirm. He announced plans to hold wolf hearings in Boise and Grangeville, one of the most wolf-hating rural towns in central Idaho. I attended the hearing in Grangeville. Two hundred people came, and Bart O'Gara and I were the only pro-wolf people to testify. The superintendent of the local grade school set the tone by pleading with Craig to stop wolf recovery now. He pointed out that many of the local school bus stops were in remote areas, so local children might become wolf fodder.

In fact, there's never been a verified case of a wild wolf's seriously injuring a person anywhere in North America. That a community leader was so badly misinformed showed me just how much work conservationists still had to do to educate the public about these animals.

I don't remember what I said at the hearing. I do recall that boos and hisses frequently interrupted my words. Of course, this crowd would have angrily denounced even the "Gettysburg Address." If this was Representative Craig's warning shot, he'd certainly caught my attention. He'd hardly dampened my desire to restore wolves to places where they belong. But the reception he'd arranged in Grangeville made it clear that wolf advocates needed to pay more attention to the political and social aspects of endangered species protection. Craig had given me a refresher course in what Les Pengelly, my old college professor, had called biopolitics.

At the same time Craig was holding his public wolf lynchings, other members of Congress were working on a proposed amendment to the Endangered Species Act that would profoundly affect wolf restoration in central Idaho and Yellowstone Park.

Unlike Craig and Symms, many members of Congress believed that the Endangered Species Act wasn't doing enough to restore imperiled wildlife. And, in truth, conservationists didn't have many success stories to which they could point. Critical reintroduction efforts had languished because of intense local resistance. Pro-wildlife politicians often pointed to stalled attempts at restoring the gray wolf to the northern Rockies and the red wolf to the southeastern United States as prime examples of this problem. Lawmakers noted that people were more afraid of the law than of the animals themselves, that they often saw the act as inflexible and contrary to their interests. Joe Helle's rantings certainly reinforced that criticism.

Pragmatic lawmakers and conservationists proposed a new

approach. They reasoned that the people most affected by endangered species restoration might cooperate more if Congress eased unnecessary Endangered Species Act restrictions and agencies tailored plans to meet specific local needs. So, Congress devised an "experimental population" provision that gave agencies considerable flexibility in crafting endangered species reintroduction programs. The only constraint of this new provision was that all plans had to result in the recovery of the species. In 1982, Congress amended the Endangered Species Act to reflect these guiding principles.

Few people at the time understood just how significant the experimental population provision of the Endangered Species Act would prove to be. Within a few years, it made restoring red wolves to North Carolina a reality. One day, it would also break the deadlock over restoring gray wolves to Yellowstone Park and central Idaho.

SIX

ASK DR. WOLF

With fear as my copilot, I eased my car into a parking space in front of the small schoolhouse in St. Anthony, Idaho. I'd arranged to discuss Yellowstone Park wolf restoration with ranchers who held livestock grazing leases on southeastern Idaho public lands bordering the park. It was 1984, and during the past seven years, I'd tangled with many of these same ranchers over predator-control issues and grizzly bear management.

It was as if I'd invited a bunch of people to a barbecue, knowing I'd be turning on the spit. Why had I done such a foolhardy thing? For two reasons. First, I thought that if ranchers understood both the rationale and plan for restoring wolves to Yellowstone Park, it might allay some of their fears. Second, I've always believed that the first step in solving a problem is to listen carefully to your adversaries. I needed to understand their concerns so I could address them. Yellowstone Park wolf restoration was unlikely to affect directly more than one hundred ranchers, and I was determined to speak with as many of them as possible.

Setting up the meetings had been easy. I'd called the Forest Service to get the addresses of all livestock producers with grazing leases on public lands within fifty miles of the park. Then I'd sent a letter to each of them. I'd set up meetings in Livingston, Montana; Cody, Wyoming; and St. Anthony. This was my first one.

I walked into the school unsure what the attendance would be. Fifteen or twenty men wearing cowboy hats lay in wait for me. On one hand, I was pleased with the turnout. On the other, I felt badly outnumbered. The mood was tense.

One deeply weathered face I recognized right away belonged to an old-time woolgrower wearing OshKosh overalls. He'd always seemed the kind of man who'd fight a rattlesnake with his bare hands and spot it three bites.

Just as I was about to launch into my spiel, the old man stood up, squinted at me in mock disbelief, and bellowed: "Hank Fischer! You mean no one's kill't you yet?" The others roared at this affirmation of our adversarial roles, and we got down to business.

Most of the ranchers had based their opinions of wolves on the frequently antagonistic controversy over grizzly bear management. So, I began by explaining how wolves are unlike grizzlies. First, I said, wolves don't attack people. I trotted out that statistic about no one's ever having been seriously hurt by a wild wolf in all of North America. This means we don't need the kind of restrictions designed to keep people and bears apart, I told the group. Second, wolves aren't attracted to people food. They're afraid of humans, so they won't bother campers or get into garbage. Third, wolves have a much higher reproduction rate than grizzlies. So, individual wolves aren't as important to the overall population as individual grizzly bears. This difference translates into greater latitude in killing animals that attack livestock.

My mere reference to the cattle issue set the room buzzing. One rancher called the wolf a bigger, stronger, more aggressive coyote that would lay waste to his livestock. I was ready for that one. I told them that annual livestock loss rates in Minnesota amount to a fraction of

1 percent.

But Minnesota isn't a good example, they insisted; the farms there are much smaller and the livestock under closer supervision than in the West. I countered that livestock loss studies in Alberta, Canada—where livestock practices are quite similar to those in Idaho, Montana, and Wyoming—reflect loss rates comparable to Minnesota's.

I had my facts down, but I wasn't winning many converts.

The questions got harder. One rancher stood up and made an impassioned speech. "It's easy to be a wolf-lover," he said. "It doesn't cost anything. It's the rancher who ends up paying the bills for wolf recovery. Who pays for my livestock when they get killed by your wolves?" I explained that in Minnesota, the state government compensates ranchers for verifiable losses to wolves and that we hoped to develop a similar program for the Yellowstone area. With a snort, the rancher responded, "Hope is a good breakfast, but it's a mighty poor supper."

Another rancher demanded to know whether he'd be able to shoot wolves he found killing his livestock. Sweat began to prickle my forehead. I went with the truth. "The Endangered Species Act doesn't permit private individuals to kill listed species unless their safety is threatened," I told him. "Because wolves aren't dangerous to humans, that's not an issue. If wolves attack your livestock, state or federal officials will come and handle the problem by either killing or moving the wolf."

The ranchers groaned in unison. One asked, "You mean if I'm with my sheep up on my allotment at Two-Top and a wolf starts laying into my ewes, I have to ride my horse out for two days in order to call some government bureaucrat who probably won't come for another three days? What if it's on a weekend?"

I resorted to my best defense, aware that it was inadequate. "The likelihood of wolves' killing livestock in the first place is darned low," I said. More groans. "The likelihood that you'll be there when it happens is even slimmer."

I got off the hook when the old woolgrower in the overalls headed off in a new direction.

"You need to understand one thing," he said. "It's not the wolf we're really worried about. We can deal with him if we need to. What we're concerned about are all the restrictions on how we do our business that come along with the wolf."

It was another tough question, one to which I didn't yet know the complete answer. I gave the best response I could. "What wolves need mostly is a good supply of deer and elk and for people not to shoot them on sight. If there's anything to do with wildlife we've done a good job with in the West," I said, "it's deer and elk. Their populations are at record highs—probably higher than since Lewis and Clark came through. We shouldn't need a whole bunch of new restrictions." My lack of specifics gave them little reassurance.

It was time to end the meeting. I felt bruised. I asked the usual final question: "Does anybody have anything else he wants to ask?" The old man in the back put up his hand.

"Yeah, I have a question," he said. "What's the best caliber to shoot the dirty beasts with, anyway?"

After the meeting, several of the ranchers thanked me for coming. One observed, "You may not be very smart, but I give you credit for having the backbone to come talk to us." I took it as progress when a couple of them said we should talk some more later.

The ranchers may not have learned much, but I learned plenty. Most of all, I realized that to be persuasive, I'd need better answers to their questions. I wasn't the only wolf advocate with that problem, either. The only person I'd seen handle such hostile crowds effectively was Dave Mech.

I first saw him in action at a wolf recovery team meeting in Boise, Idaho, where he gave a talk on wolf management in Minnesota. His formal presentation was solid, but he really excelled in fielding questions from the audience. Several ranchers who'd been invited to the meeting peppered him with hostile questions. He always gave direct, concrete answers. His mixture of science and practicality seemed bulletproof. He clearly was someone I needed to get to know better.

A middle-aged man, Mech has a dark beard and a bald head. His slanting eyes and arched eyebrows give him a predatory look that suits his line of work. He dresses for utility, not show. But it's a mistake to attribute his indifference to fashion to a lack of sophistication.

I found him to be an accessible, willing mentor without a pretentious bone in his body. He has a graduate student's enthusiasm for his work, and his excitement and fascination with science are infectious. His mind works fast. Curiosity is in his blood. "My father was a laborer with a grade-school education," he once told me. "But he had an absolutely incredible curiosity about the natural world."

Perhaps it was his blue-collar father who also instilled in Mech a down-to-earth, practical approach to issues that makes it as easy for him to talk with ranchers as with scientists. He views his work as fun—especially the field work, which takes him around the world—and admits to being a workaholic.

A private person, Mech doesn't reveal his thoughts easily. Like other scientists, he also has an exaggerated sense of objectivity. Sometimes, exasperated, I'd ask him, "How do you *feel* about this?" Sounding like *Star Trek's* Mr. Spock, he'd respond, "Why does that matter?"

It's not that he's shy about taking stands on critical issues. He thinks it's important for scientists to do so. But he worries that his professional credibility would be compromised if he became too engaged in making ethical pronouncements. He also fears that his high profile might make his judgments carry more weight than they should.

Because he has more than thirty years of experience studying wolves, when Dave Mech speaks, the scientific community listens. Besides being one of the original researchers for the famed Isle Royale wolf studies, he's studied wolf-prey relationships in Minnesota for over two decades. His 1970 book, *The Wolf,* is the definitive book on the biology of wolves. He went on to research wolves in Alaska's Denali

Park (where Adolph Murie studied the wolves of Mount McKinley) and on Ellesmere Island, in the Canadian Arctic. He has appeared on National Geographic Society television specials and has long chaired the wolf specialists' group of the prestigious World Conservation Union, formerly the International Union for Conservation of Nature and Natural Resources. The late Canadian wolf expert Douglas Pimlott was the only other scientist ever to hold this post.

I quickly discovered that Mech knows far more about wolves than he's written down. It took only a few hours with him for me to recognize the breadth of his knowledge.

I pumped him for facts and insights about wolves—anything that might help win acceptance for them in Yellowstone Park. I started by quizzing him about the Isle Royale studies, the most intensive wolf research that scientists have ever conducted. How had they influenced the way people think about wolves?

He likened the study to the story of the blind man and the elephant. "For the first years of the study," he said, "I was a blind man, and Isle Royale was the elephant. I felt a part of the elephant and drew conclusions. Then the next student came along for three years and felt another part of it, and so on. It was not until maybe the last five or ten years of the study—which started in 1958—that it became clear that each of us students was only seeing parts of the elephant. We still are only seeing parts, but we have a much more complete view now."

He explained that, when he started his Isle Royale study in 1958, it appeared that wolves and moose were in equilibrium. The wolf population seemed constant—a single pack of twenty to twenty-five animals—and moose numbers were stable. He and others tagged this situation "a balance of nature," and the press loved it. The concept became a household expression in the 1960s.

But the Isle Royale wolf-prey situation changed in ways the public still doesn't fully comprehend, he said. Throughout the 1970s, the wolf population grew, splitting into three packs totaling almost fifty animals at one point. Then the wolf population crashed—so low in the late 1980s that researchers feared that wolves might eventually disappear from Isle Royale. Now the wolves have started to build up again and level off close to twenty animals again.

So, what do these trends mean? Mech explained that moose numbers built up gradually during the early years of the study, eventually almost doubling. Wolf populations, however, remained stable. It was clear, on Isle Royale, at least, that a prey population can escape the impact of a predator; wolves, even when their numbers were greatest, didn't limit increases in moose populations.

The critical event, Mech said, was a series of hard winters that made moose vulnerable to predation. The wolves cashed in; they killed a lot of moose, sometimes leaving partly eaten carcasses to kill more. The wolf population boomed.

I asked whether that contradicted the old axiom that wolves take only the weak, the sick, or the old and that they use every bone and sinew of their prey.

"It's not always true that wolves take only what they need," he said. "They normally take what they can get, and most of the time it's barely what they need. But the part about wolves' only killing those that are predisposed to be killed—this circumstance tends to prove the point. Before the hard winters, moose could escape the wolves. The poor weather made those moose vulnerable, and the wolves were able to take advantage of it."

So, what's the lesson of Isle Royale? It's that the balance of nature isn't really very balanced at all, Mech said. Predator and prey populations always fluctuate, sometimes wildly, largely in response to weather. It was this complexity that early biologists looking at the Kaibab deer incident—including Aldo Leopold—failed to understand.

I asked him one of the questions I'd stumbled over at my meeting with ranchers in St. Anthony: Managing an endangered predator is a lot different from managing an endangered butterfly; butterflies never prey on livestock. What makes you think the Endangered Species Act contains the flexibility to manage both?

"In Minnesota, where the wolf is listed as 'threatened,' we've been taking wolves—killing them when they are proven livestock killers—for several years," he said. "We've had complete flexibility and really no hindrance. If there's a problem with wolves' killing livestock, we're able to take care of it."

At that time, in an average year, wildlife managers in Minnesota killed more than twenty-five wolves (the number is between one hundred forty and one hundred sixty now). He said the record was unclouded; when ranchers had a problem with wolves and livestock, wolves were killed.

Killing wolves was an unpleasant thought, considering that my organization's main purpose was to conserve them. But, given the wolf's blemished reputation among western stockmen, it was crucial that restoration advocates give credible assurances to ranchers that stock-killing wolves would be removed or destroyed.

I told Mech that Yellowstone-area ranchers weren't entirely comforted by my saying the government would kill problem wolves. They'd prefer to handle matters themselves. In the interest of reducing ranchers' fear, wouldn't it be better if the law let private citizens kill wolves under appropriate circumstances?

"In some cases, it might be," he replied. "But most [livestock] producers would rather have us do it. After all, it takes time and effort to go after wolves, and they'd rather have the government do it." And, unfortunately, allowing ranchers to shoot wolves is a difficult thing to regulate. "If private citizens were allowed to kill wolves," he explained, "it would be hard to know when they killed a wolf whether it was really in the area where they had a problem or five miles away. All in all, it would be difficult to manage."

Then there was the point opponents raised at every meeting: "We're not afraid of the wolf; it's restrictions on logging, grazing, or mining that come along with it we're worried about."

Mech offered loads of ammunition with which to shoot holes in that lament.

"Once wolves are established, I don't think we'll see much need to alter present land-use practices in order to protect them," he said. "Wolves should be able to live in places like Yellowstone with minimal restrictions on park activities or visitor use."

The same holds true outside the park, he added. "Some may disagree, but I would think for Yellowstone, at least, if there's some negative impact on the wolf outside the park caused by excessive road-building or whatever, there should be enough wolves within the park to resupply those wolves lost through land uses on the outside."

He said there had been no restrictions on grazing leases in Minnesota to accommodate wolves, and only temporary restrictions against timber cutting. The Forest Service rarely limited logging there and did so only when biologists had found active wolf dens right next to cutting areas. Even then, the restrictions lasted only a month.

Mech also was quick to point out that Yellowstone Park wolves probably would cause fewer problems than those in Minnesota. In Minnesota, he explained, farms and ranches are interspersed through-out much of the 31,000 square miles of wolf range—a situation maximizing chances of wolf depredation. By contrast, the 2.2-million-acre national park adjoins several huge blocks of wilderness. Sure, he said, livestock do graze on the periphery, but most of Yellowstone Park and environs contain no potential conflicts.

"I've never seen an area with a denser prey base," he said. "This is another good reason why it's likely that livestock conflicts will be few. There should be little reason for wolves to turn to livestock."

But wait a minute, I said. Cows are bigger, dumber, and slower than elk or deer. Wouldn't wolves take them because they're easier?

Mech said his research, as well as studies by other biologists in Canada, showed otherwise. "Unless wolves learn to take livestock or to recognize livestock as a legitimate prey, they don't seem to know how to handle it," he said. "In other words, they seem to prefer to hunt the prey they traditionally have been hunting. In this case, it would be primarily elk."

Mech convinced me we could adequately address the concerns

raised by Yellowstone-area ranchers. This was doable. More important, he reinforced my sense that restoring wolves to the park was the right thing to do. He was enthusiastic about the prospect.

"Yellowstone Park is a place that literally begs to have wolves," he said. "It's teeming with prey; it used to have wolves; and all the species that were there originally should be restored. Wolves would add an element to the ecosystem that would restore it to a more natural state, that would allow the public to better enjoy the park. The only thing missing in Yellowstone is the wolf, and the park can't really be wild without it. It's not a complete or natural wilderness to have all the species of prey that are there and not have the main predator they evolved with."

SEVEN

CATCHING THE WAVE

Dave Mech may have seen Yellowstone Park as a place begging to have wolves, but in the early 1980s, top officials of the Park Service weren't exactly pleading with anyone to bring them back.

What a difference a few years can make. In 1980, Americans elected Ronald Reagan president. His political revolution included appointing anti-environmental ideologue James Watt secretary of the interior, the department that oversees the Park Service. Watt, with his clear-cut head and thick glasses, became the man whose face launched a thousand cartoons. Unfortunately, his considerable influence also sank dozens of good plans, including any immediate intentions the Park Service had of restoring wolves to Yellowstone Park.

Even though it lacked support at the highest levels, the Fish and Wildlife Service continued its work on the wolf recovery plan, as the endangered species law required. Just as that agency began circulating its plan for public review, the Park Service sprang a surprise. One of its officials disclosed that the Park Service was forsaking any immediate attempt to restore wolves. In a January 1984 interview published in Montana's *Livingston Enterprise* newspaper, Yellowstone Park Chief Ranger Thomas Hobbs called wolf reintroduction a "very dim" prospect, saying that recovery plans were "definitely on the back burner." He added, "Wolves are down on the list of priorities at the moment. I couldn't even begin to predict when things would begin to roll."

Hobbs's comments struck a body blow to conservationists who'd assumed that the Park Service supported Yellowstone Park wolf restoration. After all, the agency was a member of the recovery team drafting plans for reintroducing wolves to the park, and its representative on the team had never expressed Hobbs's sentiments.

I felt deceived and angry. I wrote a letter to Yellowstone Park Superintendent Bob Barbee telling him that the Park Service's new position was ill-advised and illegal. "The Endangered Species Act doesn't instruct federal agencies to recover endangered species only when it's convenient, when it fits with other programs, or when the political climate is right," my letter read. I reminded him that the law demands that federal agencies use "all methods and procedures necessary" to removing species from the endangered list—including reintroduction, if need be. At that stage in my environmental career, I thought the law alone was enough to save wildlife.

Conservationists weren't insensitive to the political delicacies of wolf restoration, I told Barbee, but we did expect at least incremental progress. "We're asking to see positive steps to get such a program under way," I wrote. "We simply can't accept the Park Service's current position of placing wolf recovery on the back burner." In closing, I asked to meet with him to discuss the issue further.

A few weeks later, I was in Barbee's office at Yellowstone Park headquarters, in Mammoth. Most conservationists had high regard for Barbee, a large, friendly, no-nonsense guy. He surprised me by declaring at the start of our meeting that he was sympathetic to restoring wolves to the park. "But the bureaucracy seldom rewards adventurism," he said. Then he gave me a lesson in "Wolf Politics

101."

He handed me a transcript of a hearing held a few months earlier before the U.S. House of Representatives Subcommittee on Public Lands and National Parks. He'd highlighted several sentences from an exchange between Representative Larry Craig of Idaho and G. Ray Arnett, assistant secretary of the interior for fish and wildlife and parks. Arnett oversaw the Park Service. Russell Dickenson, director of the Park Service, also participated.

I read the report. Congressman Craig played the role of inquisitor, and his topic was Yellowstone Park wolf restoration: "We have been told for some time there would be no reintroduction. We now are being told there will be or there could be potential reintroduction. I have no trouble with you introducing gray wolves to Yellowstone if you first build a chain-link fence so the gray wolf doesn't come down into Idaho and into the livestock-producing areas of my state where he or she may well become a problem. That's the concern we have at this time."

Arnett and Dickenson took their cue. They played the role of loyal subjects.

"I think we have made that policy very clear that there was going to be no introduction of the wolf into Yellowstone at this time," Arnett said.

Dickenson chimed in with the exact words Craig wanted to hear: "Let me assure you, however, that because of insurmountable problems, the kind of conflicts that would occur with park neighbors, that there is no active proposal afoot and none that we can foresee in the immediate future."

When I'd finished reading, Barbee told me he cared far less about Craig's concerns than he did about those of his Park Service bosses and Senators Alan Simpson and Malcolm Wallop of Wyoming, who had more clout over matters affecting Yellowstone Park. He recounted a recent conversation with Senator Wallop, in which Barbee had gently noted that an increasing number of people were talking about restoring the wolf to Yellowstone Park. Barbee said that, in the midst of what had been a friendly meeting, Wallop froze in his chair, looked him in the eye, and said, "I don't want you to utter the 'W' word. Don't even think the 'W' word."

Having spelled out the political realities of wolf restoration, Barbee closed our meeting with some candid advice: before Yellowstone Park wolf restoration could succeed, conservation groups and government agencies would have to build both public and political support. Public support would lead to political support, he said.

He also introduced me to John Varley, the new chief of research at Yellowstone Park. Barbee had hired him to revitalize the park's floundering research program. Battles over elk and grizzly bear management had eroded public confidence in the work of park scientists. Critics complained that study results, which park managers used to make important policies, were biased because the Park Service relied too often on its own researchers rather than independent scientists.

Varley used to be a fisheries biologist, and protecting native species had long been a central part of his professional ethic. Early in his tenure, he began efforts in Yellowstone Park to restore two indigenous fish in serious trouble, the arctic grayling and cutthroat trout. In time, he also became a key ally in the wolf battles.

Years later, Varley told me the story of how he and Barbee decided to make wolf restoration a park priority. They were driving late at night to a meeting a few hours from the park. Because of fading eyesight and abundant deer near the highway, neither liked driving after dark. But Varley recalled that it was a glorious night, with stars blazing over the Beartooth Mountains. As they drove, the two men launched into a heart-to-heart discussion of what Yellowstone Park's agenda should be for the near future.

Barbee was a strategic thinker. He said to Varley, "I can focus on only a few issues in the next few years and still be effective. What do you think those issues should be?"

Varley started right in on wolf restoration. Barbee countered strongly. They argued heatedly for nearly an hour. Varley's initial impression was that Barbee had "almost a visceral negativity" to the issue of wolf recovery. The conversation lagged. Varley thought it pointless to continue. Both sat silently in the dark as they whizzed through the mountains.

Suddenly, Barbee turned to Varley and said, "Okay, let's do it. I'd like to do that."

It was only later that Varley understood Barbee's tactics. "He was testing me," Varley said. "He wanted to see for himself if I could handle the tough questions. He also wanted to gauge the depth of my passion, to see if I'd stick with it when things got tough."

Varley and Barbee already had decided to make wolf restoration a high priority by the time I met with the park superintendent. But Barbee's interest in wolves hadn't stripped him of his pragmatic concerns about political obstacles to restoration. I'd left my meeting with him unsure of the park's commitment to wolf restoration. I'd also left thinking about his suggestion that wolf advocates needed to focus more on building public support. Barbee's words had made me realize that conservationists were so focused on the fine points of the wolf recovery plan that we weren't seeing the big picture. Our strategy needed to change.

After the meeting with Barbee, I came up with one idea right away. I called Stephen Kellert, a Yale University professor and a member of Defenders of Wildlife's board of directors. He'd recently finished an exhaustive survey of public attitudes toward wolves in Minnesota. He told me that the results surprised him: Wolf support was strong throughout Minnesota, even in rural areas. Every interest group surveyed, except farmers and ranchers, supported wolf recovery.

Soon after our conversation, I asked the director of the University of Montana Environmental Studies Program whether a graduate student might be interested in surveying Yellowstone Park visitors' attitudes toward wolves. Indeed, one was. Graduate student David McNaught jumped at the chance. By the fall of 1985, he'd finished his master's thesis: an intensive attitude survey showing that 74 percent of park visitors thought "having wolves in the park would improve the Yellowstone experience." Sixty percent agreed that "if wolves can't return to Yellowstone on their own, then we should put them back ourselves." The responses to every question McNaught asked park visitors encouraged wolf restoration. His was the first of many public opinion surveys demonstrating substantial national and local backing for wolf recovery.

Another opportunity to build public support knocked not long after my meeting with Barbee. The Science Museum of Minnesota had invested five years and nearly one million dollars in creating a world-class *Wolves and Humans* exhibit. Supported by a grant from the National Endowment for the Humanities, the exhibit examined the biology of the wolf and people's attitudes toward the species. Viewers hailed it as one of the best natural history exhibits ever developed in the United States.

A few weeks later, on a trip back to Washington, D.C., I stopped in Minneapolis to see the exhibit. Although it was a weekday, visitors jammed the museum. Hordes of enthusiastic schoolchildren trooped through. Adults spent hours soaking up the smallest details. The exhibit had something for everyone: computer games simulated wolves capturing their prey; a "howling booth" encouraged visitors to imitate the howl of a wolf (a good howl elicited a response); and a central display showed ten wolves surrounding their prey, a freshly killed white-tailed deer. The individual wolves—all full-body taxidermic mounts—stood in classic positions of wolf behavior: dominance, submission, feeding, playing, scent-marking, and howling. Television monitors around the display showed footage of live wolves engaged in the same kinds of behavior. I was impressed; the exhibit was the perfect vehicle for promoting public understanding of wolves. And understanding was the first step to acceptance.

I'd arranged to meet with the museum director, who told me the exhibit would be on tour across the United States for the next several years. He said many of the nation's museums— including the National Geographic Society's Explorers Hall in Washington, D.C., and New York City's American Museum of Natural History—had already reserved the exhibit for three months or more apiece. Competition for the exhibit was stiff.

The *Wolves and Humans* loan fee was $25,000, not exactly small change for a medium-sized national conservation organization like Defenders of Wildlife. However, museum staff members made it clear they'd give priority to areas where wolf restoration was under consideration. It was expensive, but it seemed a good investment. Defenders tentatively reserved the exhibit for sites in Yellowstone Park and Boise, Idaho.

The reservations were tentative because the Park Service hadn't yet agreed to provide exhibit space in the park. Yellowstone Park managers feared that critics would accuse them of promoting wolf recovery. Fortunately, the exhibit was studiously objective. Designed to inform rather than persuade, *Wolves and Humans* sought to compel viewers to examine how they felt about wolves and then compare their perceptions with reality. The exhibit was ahead of its time in recognizing that people could go overboard both in loving and in hating wolves.

Conservationists and wolf recovery team members lobbied Superintendent Barbee relentlessly to find a place for the wolf exhibit in Yellowstone Park. But bringing wolves to Yellowstone Park in any form—even mounted animals in a museum display—aroused passions. Ultimately, Barbee stuck his neck out and said yes. *Wolves and Humans* opened in the park in June 1985. It was a smash hit. By September, it had attracted over 215,000 visitors, including new Secretary of the Interior Donald Hodel.

Although building public support for wolf restoration was our main goal, the exhibit's most important convert was the Park Service itself. After three months of answering enthusiastic visitors' questions about wolves, Park Service employees and administrators began to catch the wave: why not restore the wolf?

For years, many park rangers, interpreters, and middle managers had quietly advocated wolf reintroduction. Now it seemed acceptable to do so openly. This new Park Service commitment to wolf recovery was personified by Norm Bishop, a Yellowstone Park interpreter. He became the park's most dedicated wolf advocate, giving hundreds of talks and sending out thousands of information packets to interested citizens.

The agency's change of heart can't be attributed entirely to the exhibit. Good luck may have played an even larger role.

In the 1984 presidential election, Ronald Reagan buried Walter Mondale to win a second term. Park Service Director Russell Dickenson retired, and conservationists braced themselves for Reagan to replace him with a hard-boiled anti-environmentalist. Instead, the president appointed his old friend William Penn Mott, Jr., who ultimately did more to advance Yellowstone Park wolf restoration than any other agency leader before or since. Mott had been parks chief in California when Reagan was governor. No one knows whether Reagan realized how vigorously his appointee would protect national parks and defend their wildlife.

In many ways, Mott and Reagan were kindred spirits. Both were in their mid-seventies, energetic, extremely amiable, and not the least bit detail-oriented. "It was hard not to love the guy," John Varley once told me, referring to Mott. "Here he was, a lifelong bureaucrat, a man in his seventies yet still pure of heart. That spirit's usually been long beaten out of government employees by that time."

Mott first toured Yellowstone Park as Park Service director in early 1985. As always when top brass visited, Yellowstone Park administrators pulled out all the stops. They wanted to give their new boss a good look at the park as well as a thorough briefing on park issues. There was a lot of material to cover. Varley and others spent days preparing their presentations, boiling everything down to the essential points, with lots of charts and graphs designed to speed things along. They knew from experience to expect short attention spans from political appointees running the park system.

They brought Mott to a small log cabin on the shore of Yellowstone Lake and launched into presentations on elk, wolves, and grizzly bears and the controversy that managing these species generated. The discussion had scarcely begun when Mott became animated. He jumped out of his seat, brimming with enthusiasm. Forget the charts and graphs. Mott grasped the merits of the park's bear and elk policies and wolf restoration instantly, and he quickly offered his solution to the controversy. The problem wasn't biology, he said, but people. The Park Service simply wasn't getting its message across to the public. He proposed a massive public education campaign to make people understand, for example, why wolves belong in Yellowstone Park.

Within the week, Mott dispatched to Yellowstone Park a team of public-education specialists from the Park Service center at Harpers Ferry, West Virginia. Their arrival sent an important signal: Mott was serious; wildlife restoration wasn't just a passing fancy.

I first met Mott in June 1985 at a special preview of the *Wolves and Humans* exhibit in Yellowstone Park. Throughout his tour of the exhibit, he gestured excitedly; he was enthralled. As he sped around, he sounded what would become a familiar theme: "We need more public education. We need to do more to reach the public." He saw the exhibit as an ideal way to get the public involved in wolf restoration.

Afterward, I sat down with him and Barbee to discuss Yellowstone Park wolf restoration. Renée Askins and Timm Kaminski also attended the meeting. Askins had been heavily involved in bringing the exhibit to Yellowstone Park. Defenders had hired her to write a grant proposal that helped cover the rental costs, and the Park Service later offered her and Kaminski summer jobs as interpretive specialists at the exhibit. Both accepted.

Mott needed no prompting. He was unabashedly supportive. In his mind, bringing back the wolf was simply the right thing to do. I glanced over at Barbee, who had the look of a man being led over a cliff. Mott seemed indifferent to the perils of adventurism. The ever-pragmatic Barbee tried to bring Mott back to earth by pointing out the formidable opposition wolf recovery faced from the livestock industry and its congressional supporters. Barbee, too, wanted wolves back in Yellowstone Park, but he was more realistic about the difficulties involved.

Mott never slowed down. Instead, he waved his arms and did what he did best: he offered some advice. It seemed to come off the top of his head, but it was the most foresighted piece of wolf wisdom anyone's ever given me. He said, "The single most important action conservation groups could take to advance Yellowstone wolf recovery would be to develop a fund to compensate ranchers for any livestock losses caused by wolves." Economics makes them hate the wolf, he explained. Pay them for their lost livestock, and the controversy would subside.

Mott's enthusiasm was contagious. I left the meeting energized. My mind raced ahead. Once the wolf recovery plan was completed— probably in the next year—the Park Service would take the next step required under federal law. It would prepare an environmental impact statement laying out the various alternatives for wolf reintroduction. I figured that that might take another year. That would put wolves on the ground in Yellowstone Park within two or three years.

But, then, my friends always said I was a little optimistic.

Years of public involvement preceded attempts to capture and release wolves into Yellowstone.
Not everybody favored the return of the wolf.

The capture site near Hinton, Alberta, Canada—not the rugged mountainous terrain many might expect.

Biologist shooting wolves with a tranquilizer gun from a helicopter.

Helicopter lands near the tranquilized wolf and transports the animal back to a base camp.

Biologists carefully fitting a radio color on the muzzled
and blindfolded wolf.

Biologist checking the pulse of one of the two female wolves he is transporting back to the base camp.

Biologist carefully taking blood samples, vaccinating, weighing, and generally checking the condition of the wolf before allowing transport.

After getting a thorough physical examination, the wolves were placed in small containers for transport.

After a long flight and a ride in a converted horse trailer, the wolves symbolically pass under the Theodore Roosevelt arch at the North Entrance to Yellowstone National Park.

Transporting the wolves to the temporary holding pens.

Fish and Wildlife Service Director Mollie Beattie (*center*),
Interior Secretary Bruce Babbitt (*far right*), and
Yellowstone National Park Superintendent Mike Finley
(*back right*) help carry the wolves to the holding pens.

Wolves check out their new, but temporary, environment.

Biologists feeding road-killed deer to the wolves.

Free at last. This photo shows a wolf fleeing its recently opened transport container in central Idaho.

Lamar Valley, Yellowstone National Park, future home of the Yellowstone wolves.

EIGHT

THE GOOD, THE BAD, AND THE ENIGMATIC

A decade after passage of the 1973 Endangered Species Act, Americans had made little discernible progress in restoring *Canis lupus* to the Northern Rockies. Although a few bold wolves had sauntered into the United States on their own, most quickly succumbed to "lead poisoning"—the variety contracted from the barrel of a gun. Given the paucity of wolves roaming the Northern Rockies in 1983 and 1984, it seemed terribly ironic that the government's wolf recovery team then was spending about 80 percent of its time discussing how to kill wolves and only about 20 percent on how to protect them. I later came to appreciate that that ratio probably had been about right.

The team raised endless questions about wolf-killing. Should private landowners be allowed to shoot wolves on sight? Should federal land-management agencies establish zones where wolves receive no protection? Should Animal Damage Control or the Fish and Wildlife Service kill wolves the first time they prey on livestock, or should federal agents relocate problem animals? The team's meetings fell into a familiar pattern. John Weaver defined wolves' biological needs. Bart O'Gara injected practicality. Conservationists supplied encouragement. And Joe Helle provided fireworks. Helle merely seethed through most meetings but occasionally boiled over into a lecture.

"You pseudo-environmentalists make the wolf look like Bambi," he'd rant. "You think that he just sniffs the air and looks cute, that he doesn't tear the belly out of a living horse, that he doesn't hamstring sheep and drag them down and choke the living breath from their throats."

A recovery team member or one of the conservationists would then explain to Helle that all these wolf management discussions were taking place solely to accommodate livestock industry concerns.

I didn't dislike Helle for his outbursts. I recognized them for what they were: a skillful means of intimidation. I respected his effectiveness at representing livestock industry interests. His call to arms the previous year had caused the director of the Fish and Wildlife Service to withdraw the first draft of the wolf recovery plan. You could learn from Helle; he knew how to work the system. His surprise attack had succeeded the first time. I vowed not to get outflanked again.

By 1983, conservationists' interest in wolf recovery had expanded. Tom France, an attorney who runs the northern Rockies office of the National Wildlife Federation, began attending recovery team meetings. He had the backing of one of the nation's largest conservation organizations. Moreover, the Wildlife Federation's local affiliates—the Montana, Idaho, and Wyoming Wildlife Federations—were sportsmen's groups with considerable regional influence. France, who plays rugby in his off hours, can be an aggressive advocate when the situation demands it. Helle demanded it frequently.

Eighteen months after Helle had blown up the first plan, the wolf recovery team issued a new draft that finally addressed the critical wolf recovery issues. The November 1983 plan identified three recovery areas: northwestern Montana, central Idaho, and the Yellowstone Park area. It established a recovery goal of ten breeding pairs of wolves (a breeding pair being the essential element of a pack) for each recovery area. The plan also proposed a system of controlling wolves based on dividing each recovery area into distinct zones of protection.

Despite these breakthroughs, the plan had two gaping holes: it permitted removing the wolf from the endangered species list when only two of the three recovery areas had met their goals, and it proposed only natural recovery, not reintroduction, for Yellowstone Park.

This time, conservationists hit the copy machines first and with even more zeal than Helle had in round one. We swamped the recovery team with letters and phone calls in which we insisted on a stronger plan. The team felt the pressure.

The decisive recovery team meeting took place in March 1984 in Missoula. The first issue was whether the plan would require wolf recovery in just two areas or all three. It didn't take a genius to know that Yellowstone Park would get dropped if it were only two. After all, it would be far simpler for wolves to colonize northwestern Montana and central Idaho, the two areas nearest existing Canadian wolf populations. Weaver saved the day by pointing out that the grizzly bear recovery plan called for restoration in a minimum of four areas. For consistency's sake, he reasoned, the Northern Rockies wolf recovery plan should include at least three areas. Team members concurred, and the change easily won approval.

The big debate concerned Yellowstone Park: to reintroduce or not to reintroduce, that was the question. The team had been heading toward this showdown for three years. Team leader Bart O'Gara led the way by casting his vote against Yellowstone Park reintroduction. He thought it controversial to the point of being unachievable. Ever sensible, he didn't want to pick a fight he couldn't win. O'Gara spoke from experience; for the past three years, he'd been the target of intensive sniping from the livestock industry.

Bob Ream stood up next. Everyone respected him as a wolf researcher and advocate. He wasn't one to sell the wolf short. But he, too, opposed Yellowstone Park wolf reintroduction. He reasoned that, given enough time, wolves probably would return to the park on their own. It would be easier for people to accept their reappearance this way, he said. Besides, reintroduction—capturing wolves in Canada and shipping them in—would be expensive and time-consuming. It would make more sense, Ream said, to direct scarce government funds toward existing wolf recovery research and management in the Glacier Park area.

The room was quiet. Wolf advocates glanced nervously at one another. With two of the team's most influential members opposed to the idea, it seemed as if Yellowstone Park wolf reintroduction was about to get deep-sixed. Then Weaver took the floor. He argued that the scientific case for wolves' returning to Yellowstone Park without reintroduction was weak. Glacier Park is less than one hundred fifty miles from wolf populations in Canada, he said, yet it had taken more than twenty years for wolves to bridge that gap. He questioned the likelihood that wolves would move another three hundred miles farther south anytime in the foreseeable future.

Individual wolves might journey that far, he conceded. But the odds were extremely remote that two adult wolves of opposite sexes would travel that distance, find each other, mate, and successfully raise their pups. He argued that the team's proposal to restore wolves to all three areas wasn't biologically supportable unless it endorsed Yellowstone Park reintroduction.

Weaver was persuasive. Perhaps more important, the livestock industry's uncompromising attitude and Joe Helle's hardball politics had exasperated many recovery team members. Several members believed that recovery plans should be biological documents, not political ones. The final vote came down six to five in favor of Yellowstone Park reintroduction.

In October 1985, the team produced a final draft of the plan, recommending natural wolf recovery for northwestern Montana and central Idaho and reintroduction for Yellowstone Park. The recovery team also added one important new wrinkle: agencies would reintroduce wolves to the park under the experimental population provision of the Endangered Species Act. The team submitted the document for public review, distributing it to state wildlife agencies, conservation groups, the livestock industry, newspapers, and many other outlets. Conservation groups once again rallied support, and this time 85 percent of the written public comment the Fish and Wildlife Service received was favorable.

A major stumbling block remained. Before the plan could go into effect, a high-ranking Fish and Wildlife Service official would have to sign it.

Helle and his livestock industry friends weren't eager for that day to come, of course. In a letter to their political friends, they called for congressional hearings to "determine whether endangered species programs, such as the wolf recovery plan as it is being conducted, are within the intent of the Endangered Species Act and in the best interests of the taxpaying public."

Politicians from Montana, Wyoming, and Idaho added their voices to the chorus of opposition to the recovery plan. "I think Montana needs wolves like it needs another drought," Republican Representative Ron Marlenee wrote in a column for the *Billings Gazette*. "Will the wolf be just another ploy by 'green bigots' to block economic development of Montana? Grizzly bear habitat has been used as a rationale to block ski areas, roads and much more. Environmentalists must be salivating; think of all the land that can be locked up."

Republican Senator Alan Simpson of Wyoming was equally unenthusiastic about the recovery plan. "Man and wolf have never been on very friendly terms," he observed in a news release. "In a state like Wyoming, where we rely heavily on our livestock industry, the wolf is not actually a very welcome new resident."

Republican Senator Steve Symms of Idaho warned, "Wolves are not only a threat to livestock, but pose a real danger to humans." He made this outrageous, baseless claim in a letter to a teacher who'd recently taken her class to see the *Wolves and Humans* exhibit in Boise.

In 1986, the controversy played out differently from the way it had in 1982. The ranks of wolf advocates had swelled considerably, thanks mainly to the spirited advocacy of Park Service Director Bill Mott. The issue of restoring wolves to Yellowstone Park had developed a national profile. Stories evaluating the likelihood of reintroduction appeared not only in national conservation publications like *Audubon, Natural History,* and *Defenders* but also in major media outlets like *The Washington Post, The New York Times,* and *Newsweek.* Conservationists had started to accomplish part one of Bob Barbee's advice: build public support.

We struggled with Barbee's second piece of counsel: build political support. Conservation leaders realized that the recovery plan would sit on the shelf without political backing from the region: Montana, Idaho, and Wyoming. It's an unwritten political law that members of Congress don't intrude on the affairs of another member's state. The only breach of that rule in recent memory occurred when the landmark Alaska lands bill, protecting millions of acres as wilderness and parks, passed over the protests of the Alaska congressional delegation. The support of fifty members of Congress from the East Coast wouldn't count as much as the support of a single member from the Northern Rockies region. We needed a wolf champion.

An assessment of the prospects was depressing. In Wyoming, our choices were Senators Malcolm Wallop and Alan Simpson or Representative Dick Cheney: all conservative Republicans, all devoutly anti-wolf. Enough said.

Montana seemed friendlier. Democratic Senators John Melcher and Max Baucus had decent environmental voting records, as did Democratic Representative Pat Williams. Representative Marlenee was the only hopeless case; in a recent newspaper story, he'd compared restoring wolves to Yellowstone Park to bringing cockroaches back to your attic. I couldn't help thinking of English poet Alexander Pope's observation that narrow-necked bottles are like narrow-minded people: the less they have in them, the more noise they make pouring it out.

I tried lobbying Senator Melcher. A former veterinarian, he had a soft spot in his heart for animals. Unfortunately, he had an even softer spot for livestock industry acquaintances he'd made while working as a vet. Although I'd written him several letters and visited him twice, Melcher remained staunchly anti-wolf.

On the surface, Senator Baucus seemed the most probable source of support. He had a solid environmental record, and we had a good working relationship. But I also knew that Baucus's family owns the biggest sheep ranch in Montana and that his father was one of the Montana Wool Growers Association's most outspoken opponents of predators.

I arranged a meeting with Baucus at his Hart Senate Office Building suite on Capitol Hill. Pat Tucker, who worked with Tom France at the National Wildlife Federation's regional office in Missoula, came along. Baucus—handsome, athletic, and in his mid-forties—greeted us cheerfully. With barely a word, he whisked us into a foyer, where he had a staff photographer waiting to take a picture of the three of us. Since we'd hardly said hello, the moment seemed awkward. Tucker and I shrugged off the photo session as a technique that members of Congress use to make visitors feel important.

The meeting started off well. We made small talk about events in Montana and had a positive discussion about the future of a Montana wilderness bill, legislation Baucus supported. Then we turned to the point of the meeting: gaining his support for restoring wolves to Yellowstone Park.

I might as well have placed a dead possum on his desk. He became agitated. When Baucus gets excited, his eyes bulge. In a matter of seconds, they reminded me of the dog in Hans Christian Andersen's fairy tale "The Tinder Box": they were as big as saucers. He grumbled that reintroducing wolves to Yellowstone Park was unrealistic, frivolous, and didn't have a chance of happening; it was, in sum, an environmentalist's pipe dream. Had we spoken to anyone in the livestock industry? he demanded. By this time, his eyeballs were almost brushing my suit.

I'd anticipated that he might not respond favorably to Plan A, so I laid out Plan B. "We don't expect you publicly to endorse Yellowstone Park wolf reintroduction," I said. "We only want you to agree that agencies should follow the procedures that Congress has established for recovery of endangered species, like completing recovery plans."

I'm not even sure Baucus heard Plan B. Visibly distracted, he abruptly stood up, left the room, and didn't come back. His staff member who was also in the room shrugged his shoulders and looked puzzled. I received a nice, glossy 8" x 10" photo a few weeks later in the mail.

Next, I visited Congressman Williams, the best environmentalist in the three-state region. In fairness, I should note that this is faint praise. Still, Williams has been a solid Endangered Species Act supporter who's often gone to bat for conservationists. This time, though, he struck out. He did have the courtesy to feign interest in the support-the-process position I'd suggested to Baucus. But, clearly, he considered the topic too hot to handle. I left his office keenly aware that my search for a Yellowstone Park wolf champion couldn't be much more discouraging.

On paper, the Idaho congressional delegation looked as hopelessly anti-wolf as Wyoming's. Senator Symms and Republican Representative Larry Craig were card-carrying wolf-haters. I'd have had better luck penetrating Fort Knox. Representative Richard Stallings, a first-term Democrat, merited a visit. He was extremely cautious—the kind of person who'd wear both a belt and suspenders to hold up his pants. No luck. The wolf issue wasn't for the timid. That left only Senator Jim McClure.

The *dreaded* Jim McClure. If he wasn't the member of Congress environmentalists hated most, he certainly was the one they feared above all others. He was the best-known, most senior, and most powerful member of Congress from the three-state region. A member of Congress since 1966, McClure was the ranking Republican on the Senate Energy and Natural Resources Committee. He also was the ranking Republican on the Senate Appropriations Committee's Subcommittee on Interior and Related Agencies. That position gave him authority over the budgets of the Park Service, the Forest Service, and the Fish and Wildlife Service. He could manipulate the actions of these agencies like no one else in Congress.

McClure knew and frequently used the most effective technique for striking terror to the hearts of federal bureaucrats: he went after their budgets. Unlike Marlenee or Symms, he didn't bully agencies publicly. Instead, he inserted language into appropriations bills that brought agencies to their knees. He'd already made his opinions known on the issue of Idaho wolf recovery. In 1983, McClure slipped into the interior appropriations bill a clause prohibiting spending federal money on wolf studies outside wilderness areas. He made his move in the final hours before the vote, when Congress wouldn't have time to review the bill thoroughly. His tactic was a simple, effective way to limit the agencies' ability to protect wolf habitat. He'd taken similar actions to bend agencies to his will on grizzly bear and forest management issues.

McClure's closest friends were loggers, miners, and ranchers. For the previous two sessions of Congress, he'd received a zero score from the League of Conservation Voters, a national nonprofit group that charts congressional environmental voting records.

Conservationists probably would have written McClure off as just another wolf opponent if his main natural resources staffer, Carl Haywood, hadn't begun attending wolf recovery team meetings. Everyone on the team suspected that Haywood was up to no good. To our surprise, despite his boss's awful environmental record, he never disrupted recovery team meetings with tantrums or anti-wolf invective. His comments were constructive. At one meeting, he astonished us by announcing that Senator McClure would support wolf recovery if the agencies could develop a practical plan.

After watching Haywood in action, I began to respect his ability. He knew the legal nuances of the Endangered Species Act and understood how agencies implement the law in Montana, Idaho, and Wyoming. Congressional staffers tend to be young and inexperienced. Haywood, in his mid-fifties, understood the intricacies of government. In fact, he was one of the best-informed congressional staffers I'd ever met. His skill no doubt contributed to Senator McClure's effectiveness. I began to develop an effective working relationship with him.

Haywood and I agreed that Idaho politicians didn't understand the wolf recovery plan. I suggested we hold a meeting in Boise to educate them. He invited congressional staffers, representatives of the governor's office, and members of the livestock industry. I invited conservationists, including France, and asked Dave Mech to tell the group about wolf recovery in Minnesota.

Everyone attended. Mech gave his usual excellent presentation. The congressional staffers asked the normal questions. Conservationists and ranchers bickered about the customary problems. The wolf education process trudged on.

As often happens, the important business took place after the formal meeting was over. Haywood, adept at picking out the major players in any issue, sought out Mech for a private meeting. He and Mech share several traits: both are practical, no-nonsense people interested in solutions, not talk. They got along well. Haywood used Mech to educate himself on the biological necessities of wolf recovery. Mech used Haywood as a political sounding board.

Although Haywood's a former outfitter with an affinity for the outdoors, he's no closet wolf-lover. He shared and accurately represented McClure's interests regarding wolves and the senator's commodity-oriented constituents. What was McClure's stake in wolf recovery? The uncomplicated answer would be that wolf recovery was a highly divisive issue he believed couldn't be resolved without political leadership.

The cynical response would be that McClure, shrewder than other politicians, was looking out for the interests of his industry pals. McClure probably recognized that wolves eventually would return to Idaho whether ranchers liked it or not, and when they did, they'd enjoy the full protection of the Endangered Species Act. McClure thought environmentalists might use the law to press for land-use restrictions affecting his resource-using friends. Quite possibly, he was trying to strike a better deal before the wolves returned.

For the next several years, environmentalists argued about McClure's possible motives for supporting wolf recovery. I didn't know, and I didn't care. We'd found a regional politician willing to back wolf recovery in central Idaho and Yellowstone Park. Our good luck was that he happened to be the most powerful politician in the region. For the moment, at least, that was good enough for me.

At the urging of Tom France and me, Haywood agreed to try to set up meetings between the livestock industry and conservationists; no government people would be there. We agreed that this would be the most effective way to advance solutions to wolf management problems. But livestock industry representatives weren't interested. Their attitude was the same as Congressman Marlenee's: "No wolves, nowhere, no way."

Haywood had another idea. He said the livestock industry wouldn't negotiate because it viewed wolves and livestock as fundamentally incompatible. To change its mind, he said, we needed to show industry leaders this isn't true. Haywood suggested we take them on a field trip to Minnesota to see for themselves how livestock producers cope with wolves.

His plan seemed a good idea, but we needed some other people. I thought we should invite conservation leaders as well as Mech, the wolf expert. Haywood suggested we ask other western congressional staffers and the leader of Minnesota's Animal Damage Control program to come along, too. Almost everyone we invited accepted.

Several months, a few hundred phone calls, and more than $10,000 from Defenders of Wildlife later, a group of twenty stood in a cow pasture hacked out of Minnesota's north woods, talking about wolves and livestock and kicking gravel. It had been difficult, but we'd managed to persuade six livestock industry leaders, two from each state in the region, to join Haywood and me on the two-day field trip.

Our purpose wasn't to show the livestock industry the typical Minnesota farm. That would have been too boring. At that time—1987—fewer than two of every thousand livestock producers in Minnesota wolf range claimed losses to wolves in an average year. We showed them the worst. We visited a farm that had suffered chronic losses to wolves. Next, we had a "town meeting" with local cattle and sheep producers, some of whom had experienced the worst livestock losses to wolves in the state. We had many spirited discussions.

The livestock industry leaders repeatedly brought up one point. As the ranchers in St. Anthony, Idaho, had said in 1984, they weren't afraid of the wolf itself. But they wanted to be sure that an adequate control program was in place and that federal agencies and environmentalists wouldn't use the wolf as an excuse to lock them out of public lands.

The industry leaders were concerned that livestock producers in Minnesota couldn't kill wolves they saw attacking their livestock. Haywood and I informed them that the experimental population provision of the Endangered Species Act could permit such killing of wolves by private citizens. They wanted compensation for livestock losses as well. At the time, Minnesota paid up to $400 for each animal lost to wolves. That program wasn't good enough, they argued; they should receive market value for their stock.

The Minnesota trip didn't convert anybody, but it represented progress. It helped wolf advocates and livestock industry representatives focus on the crux of the conflict. We weren't agreeing, but at least we were talking. The trip clarified the problems that had to be solved. As Yellowstone Park Superintendent Bob Barbee had said, "Yellowstone wolf restoration won't happen unless opponents get their concerns met."

While developing these new relationships with the livestock industry, conservationists continued pressuring the Fish and Wildlife Service to sign the recovery plan and begin implementing it. The conservation community brought a full-court press against the hostile Reagan administration. We organized letter-writing campaigns. We held meetings with and eventually threatened lawsuits against the Fish and Wildlife Service. We invited Mech to Capitol Hill for informational meetings with congressional staff. We persuaded leaders of key congressional resource committees to write letters to the Fish and Wildlife Service demanding action on the recovery plan.

The plan wasn't likely to go anywhere—at least, not for a while. One major reason? In 1986, President Reagan had appointed a new Fish and Wildlife Service director: Frank Dunkle, the archenemy of my former professor Les Pengelly. I found Dunkle to be just as Pengelly had described him: an enigma. He seemed pro-wildlife but only when it was politically convenient. Dunkle had the arrogant manner of a person used to getting what he wanted. It was no wonder his employees seemed to fear him.

Dunkle reacted to conservationists' pressure on the wolf recovery plan by announcing in December 1986 that he'd give Congress, the public, and the fish and game commissions of Montana, Wyoming, and Idaho one last chance to comment on the wolf recovery plan. This would be the third public review in five years. Clearly, his intention was to give wolf opponents another chance to say no.

Conservationists seized on the comment period as an opportunity rather than an obstacle. The National Wildlife Federation, the National Audubon Society, and Defenders sent out alerts to their members, asking them to write letters supporting wolf restoration. Public comment from conservation group members and others was overwhelmingly supportive. But Dunkle still didn't approve the plan.

Conservationists were troubled. At the International Wolf Symposium, which Defenders sponsored in April 1987 in Washington, D.C., Dunkle said wolves were returning on their own to northwestern Montana and that natural recovery was a distinct possibility for Yellowstone Park. In other words, he seemed ready to reopen the whole debate over whether to reintroduce wolves. Never mind that the recovery plan sitting on his desk stated plainly that the likelihood of a viable wolf population's reestablishing itself in Yellowstone Park was "extremely remote."

Recent events fueled the urgency of putting the recovery plan into action. Wolves had begun breeding in northwestern Montana. In 1986, Bob Ream's Wolf Ecology Project had documented the first wolf reproduction in Glacier Park in nearly fifty years. By mid-1987, researchers had documented three packs totaling nearly thirty animals. One pack lived in Montana; the other two roamed the border.

People in Idaho continued to report wolf sightings as well. Timm Kaminski, who'd begun analyzing Idaho wolf sightings for the Fish and Wildlife Service in 1983, had uncovered nearly six hundred reports of sightings spanning the previous twenty years. Almost two hundred of them were listed as "probable." He'd found no evidence of reproduction, but some people thought a small wolf population might already exist in Idaho. Although scientists like Mech were highly skeptical, this optimism had led to the recovery team's recommending a natural recolonization strategy for Idaho.

Western politicians and livestock growers had fiercely opposed the recovery plan. Dunkle had dragged his heels. Nevertheless, in August 1987, the day wolf advocates had long awaited finally arrived: the recovery plan got its signature. Interestingly enough, it wasn't Dunkle's but that of the Fish and Wildlife Service acting regional director in Denver, Colorado. Many people believe that Dunkle hadn't wanted his fingerprints on the document.

Conservationists were delighted that their wish had come true. But the result spelled anything but a fairy tale ending for the animals they sought to protect. For Montana's small population of wolves, it would be their most trying year.

NINE

The Summer From Hell

One starry night in August 1987, I sat in front of a campfire along an isolated stretch of Montana's Smith River—just about my favorite place on earth. Sharing the warmth of the fire were my wife, Carol; Tom France; and another friend. That morning, we'd embarked on a fifty-five mile, four-day raft trip downriver.

It had been a clear, hot day, and the trout had chased our flies with vigor. Now, in the cool of the evening, we relaxed and exchanged barbs about our fishing prowess. France, always one for special touches, had brought the fixings for an unconventional backwoods drink: ice, vermouth, gin, and olives for martinis. Carol, who'd never drunk a martini before, gulped one down and asked for a refill. Things went downhill fast. Soon, all four of us were giggling wildly.

Suddenly, a tall man stepped out of the shadows into the ring of light cast by our fire, startling us. "I'm looking for Tom France," he said. I recognized him as the river ranger for Montana's Department of Fish, Wildlife and Parks. France stood up. "I need to take you out to where you can make a phone call," the ranger told him.

Our hearts fell. We all had the same thought: someone's dead. Had it been a car crash? A heart attack? France would know soon enough. We grimly made our plan: he'd walk out with the ranger, and if he wasn't back by nine the next morning, the three of us would go on without him.

But a few minutes before nine the next morning, France hiked down the path with a smile on his face. "Nobody's dead?" we all asked at once.

"No, but someone's going to be," he replied. Apparently, Wayne Brewster of the Fish and Wildlife Service had been trying hard to reach us. Finally, Brewster had left a message with France's assistant that sounded so urgent she'd overreacted and tried to find us in the wilds. "The wolves up near Browning are killing livestock," France explained. "Brewster says they're going to shoot them today if they can. He was just giving us a heads-up. I think he wanted some reassurance that we wouldn't sue him if they pulled the trigger."

The saga of the wolves of Browning, Montana, began in the winter of 1986. Glacier Park officials reported seeing five wolves chasing an elk across a frozen lake on the east side of the park, a short distance from Browning, a small town on the Blackfeet Indian Reservation. All previous wolf reports had been on the west side of the park, along the North Fork of the Flathead River. The two areas are only about fifty miles apart as the crow flies, but the high peaks of Glacier Park separate them.

Two women repairing fences had heard an animal bellowing. Upon searching, they discovered two gray-colored wolves killing a nine-hundred-pound cow. It was crisis time.

The Fish and Wildlife Service had drafted a plan for controlling problem wolves. It called for capturing, radio collaring, and relocating wolves after their first attack on livestock and killing or removing them to captivity after their second. Two strikes, and they'd be out.

The agency had learned from the Bearpaw Wolf ordeal. The wolf recovery plan allowed the Fish and Wildlife Service to kill wolves if necessary to stop livestock predation. The recovery team had made a difficult call, deciding to deal swiftly with problem wolves to promote conservation of the greater number of wolves that don't kill livestock. That provision had won support from conservationists.

But the Fish and Wildlife Service still had no trained personnel or any equipment for capturing wolves. Neither did Animal Damage Control, the organization the Fish and Wildlife Service called upon for help when wolves attacked livestock. An Animal Damage Control trapper tried unsuccessfully to catch the Browning wolves for several weeks. But when he became ill, there was no one to replace him. So, for nearly a month, the problem went unattended. Fortunately, the livestock killing stopped. The trapper set snares again at the end of June, and this time he hit the jackpot: he caught two wolves. One was a black wolf with only three legs; the lower part of his rear leg apparently had been shot off. The other was a large gray-colored male.

The trapper, unprepared to deal with captured wolves, had no drugs to immobilize them. Instead, he handled the problem western-style: he lassoed them, tied their legs with rope, placed a stick in their mouths, and wrapped tape around their jaws. Then he stowed them in his garage until Fish and Wildlife Service biologists arrived.

The agency scientists fitted the gray male with a radio collar and released him. They planned to follow him with radio-tracking equipment in hopes he'd lead them to the other pack members—a strategy called the "Judas" technique. The Fish and Wildlife Service decided the three-legged wolf couldn't make it in the wild and sent him to an animal research facility in Minnesota.

In early August, the wolves struck again, killing eight adult sheep and one lamb on a ranch only a few miles from their first kill. The ranchers, who at first had been patient, began to complain bitterly. "Why should we feed their damned wolves?" asked the rancher who'd lost the first cow.

"I never was a fellow that feels everything should be exterminated," another local stockman said, "but this is costing the stockgrowers too much money."

Dan Geer, the rancher who'd lost the sheep, told the *Great Falls*

Tribune, "If somebody would be willing to pay for the livestock they eat, maybe we could tolerate some of it." Geer's tolerance turned into fury when the wolves went on a rampage, killing three of his steers in one week. He wasn't a wealthy man, and he'd lost more than $2,000 worth of livestock. He got on the phone with the Fish and Wildlife Service's Wayne Brewster and yelled, "If you don't fix this problem right now, I'll kill the wolves myself and hang them on my mailbox, the government be damned."

That was the day Brewster placed the urgent phone call that led to Tom France's summons on the Smith River. Soon afterward, a helicopter carrying an Animal Damage Control agent lit out after the pack. The agent ended up gunning down the big gray wolf, which had turned out to be the primary stock killer.

But the problem wasn't resolved. Other livestock-killing wolves from the Browning pack remained at large. Tensions ran high between Animal Damage Control and the Fish and Wildlife Service. Bad feelings had developed early on when the Fish and Wildlife Service insisted that one of its employees had to be on hand whenever Animal Damage Control used the agency's radio-tracking equipment. Animal Damage Control resented the implication that its agents, left to their own devices, would use radio-tracking equipment to pull off the old rancher stunt: shoot, shovel, and shut up.

Animal Damage Control and the Fish and Wildlife Service were at odds over other matters as well. Animal Damage Control believed that it and the Fish and Wildlife Service needed to find a solution to ranchers' livestock loss problems as soon as possible. It argued that failing to act quickly and decisively would do far more to endanger future wolf recovery efforts than would killing a few animals. The Fish and Wildlife Service, sensitive to the fact that the Browning wolves were one of Montana's pioneer wolf packs, wanted to capture the animals and relocate them if possible. But neither agency had the skill or resources to make this happen in a timely way.

The Browning incident dragged on until late September. Maybe what happened to the seven-member wolf pack was inevitable: by the time Animal Damage Control and Fish and Wildlife Service agents finally left, four wolves were dead, and two had been placed in captivity. Only one wolf that couldn't be caught remained alive. But he didn't last long. It's impossible to be certain, but it's likely that someone shot him.

The goings-on in Browning seriously slowed wolf recovery momentum. Day after day, newspapers ran stories quoting angry ranchers. At the prodding of livestock associations, politicians launched congressional inquiries into the recent events. The timing of the wolves' attacks on livestock was bad, occurring just after the Fish and Wildlife Service signed the wolf recovery plan.

Conservationists watched helplessly as the Browning fiasco unfolded. It was a no-win situation for everyone. Three ranchers were angry because they'd lost valuable livestock; many in the area vowed to shoot wolves on sight in the future. Wolf advocates were upset because wolves were dead and ranchers were continuing to bad-mouth the species. The prospects for wolves in the Browning area were dim, regardless of whether they killed livestock.

The conservation groups closely involved with the issue of Montana wolf recovery—the National Wildlife Federation, the National Audubon Society, and Defenders of Wildlife—didn't oppose the Browning control efforts. Some members of our groups assailed those of us in leadership positions for not protesting the wolf killings. But we'd had to keep our word to the Fish and Wildlife Service and the livestock industry; for several years we'd been telling them that conservationists supported prompt control of wolves that had killed livestock. Keeping that promise was hard but eventually paid significant dividends.

By the end of that August, ten sheep and five cows had been lost to wolves near Browning. I found myself thinking more and more about what Dan Geer had told the *Great Falls Tribune* and what Bill Mott had suggested to me two years before in Yellowstone Park: pay the ranchers for their losses, and their tolerance for wolf predation will increase. Did stockmen instinctively despise wolves, or did economics foster the hatred? The question demanded an answer.

I'd been urging Defenders to start a private wolf compensation fund ever since Mott advised it. The trip to Minnesota with the livestock industry had strengthened my resolve. If ranchers had to bear the cost of wolf damage, they'd end up taking out their hostility on wolves. The concept seemed so simple, so logical: shift the economic responsibility associated with wolf recovery from individual livestock producers to the millions of people in the country who support wolf restoration.

Understandably, Defenders' board of directors was reluctant to assume such an uncertain financial commitment. But that was exactly the point, I argued. Ranchers oppose wolf recovery because they fear the same uncertainty. Was it fair to ask them to shoulder a burden we wouldn't carry ourselves? If we believed the scientific studies showing that livestock losses to wolves are minor, why not just pay for the losses and end the debate? Did we want to argue about the potential severity of livestock losses, or did we want to succeed in restoring wolves? Following Mott's lead, I also contended that eliminating our opponents' economic concerns might dissolve their opposition.

Some people maintained that conservationists should lobby Congress to create a *federal* wolf compensation fund. This idea made little sense to me. It would be far cheaper and more efficient to pay for livestock losses outright than to pay lobbyists for several years to push legislation that might never pass. Federal agencies had already announced their opposition to such a fund. So had important conservation groups, including the National Wildlife Federation. They feared that a government fund might set a precedent leading to federal compensation for all wildlife damage. I had little confidence that Congress would like the idea any better.

I suggested to Defenders that we conduct an experiment. We'd compensate the Browning ranchers on a one-time basis, observe the results, and decide later whether to create a permanent fund. The Defenders board agreed.

The only catch? I had to raise the three thousand dollars to pay for the lost livestock. I made a list of likely contributors and started making phone calls. The response was overwhelming. People loved the idea of assuming financial responsibility for damage done by wolves. They were tired of all the posturing and squabbling. Most believed that paying ranchers for their losses was a practical way to solve the problem. Within forty-eight hours, I had my money. In September 1987, Defenders sent checks to the ranchers who'd lost stock.

Compensating the ranchers ended the Browning story. Newspaper articles disappeared, and the controversy subsided. Paying the ranchers couldn't bring back the Browning wolves, of course, but it did change the political dynamics for wolves elsewhere in the Rockies.

Wolf politics continued to boil in the summer of 1987. While government agents dueled with the Browning wolves, Mott was locked in an intense struggle with the Wyoming congressional delegation. The wolf recovery plan, signed in early August, concluded that reintroduction was now appropriate for Yellowstone Park. Completion of this document shifted the ball from the Fish and Wildlife Service's court to the Park Service's.

Director Mott was a willing ball-carrier, the kind who'd carry the ball thirty times a game and never complain. He'd angered the Wyoming lawmakers by suggesting that an environmental impact statement on Yellowstone Park wolf restoration would be the logical way to spark public discussion and dispassionately examine the issues. Federal law requires environmental impact statements for all federal projects that might significantly affect the environment.

In response, the Wyoming congressional delegation called a high-level meeting in August to duke it out with Mott, Assistant Secretary of the Interior Bill Horn, and Fish and Wildlife Service Director Frank Dunkle. The all-Republican Wyoming delegation leaned hard on their Republican comrades in the Reagan administration; the Yellowstone Park wolf advocacy had to stop, the delegation insisted.

Mott protested, arguing that as director of the Park Service, it was his duty under the law to support restoration of native species. The group debated awhile. Then administration officials—including Mott—promised the Wyoming delegation they'd take no action to advance Yellowstone Park wolf reintroduction without the politicians' blessing.

Mott could be brought to heel but couldn't be muzzled. Only a week or so after meeting with the Wyoming politicians, he gave an extensive interview to Wyoming's leading newspaper, the Casper *Star-Tribune*. He said that most opposition to Yellowstone Park wolf restoration was political and that there was little scientific basis for most of the objections.

"I think many people have been sold on the idea that the wolf is a bad animal, that it's a wicked animal, that it's going to kill all the livestock," Mott said. "In my mind, [wolves] would add a great deal to the natural values of Yellowstone and balance the ecosystem. The wolf . . . is not only a marvelous animal, but it is a symbol of the West. For people to be able to hear a wolf howl is going to be a very exciting opportunity."

Those statements infuriated the Wyoming congressional delegation, especially Representative Dick Cheney. He fired off a scorching letter to Mott's boss, Secretary of the Interior Donald Hodel. "I just want you to know that I am every bit as committed to preventing government introduction of wolves to Yellowstone as Bill Mott is determined to put them there," Cheney declared. "If he wants to fight, I'm ready." Cheney did go on to fight, but not against wolf recovery. President George Bush drafted him to be secretary of defense in 1989, and Cheney gained national prominence for his Desert Storm leadership.

Cheney affected Mott about the same way he later affected Saddam Hussein: the short-term impact was awesome, the long-term effect insignificant. Cheney's anti-wolf missile scored a direct hit on Hodel's desk. The next day, under heavy pressure, Mott announced to the press that he was sorry if there had been misunderstandings and that Yellowstone Park wolf restoration was "on hold" until the Park Service could win the consent of the Wyoming congressional delegation.

Frank Dunkle ingratiated himself with the Wyoming delegation, dazzling its members with his skillful political maneuvering. In a September speech to Montana timber industry officials, he announced he had no plans to implement the newly signed wolf recovery document. He also said he wouldn't support reintroducing wolves to Yellowstone Park, calling such a plan "foolhardy." No one asked him why, just a month earlier, his own agency had approved a recovery plan that strongly recommended Yellowstone Park wolf reintroduction.

Dunkle next took his roadshow to Wyoming, where he spoke to the Wyoming Wool Growers Association. He told them precisely what they and the Wyoming politicians wanted to hear: "The only wolves that I will bring to Wyoming are the ones on my tie," he said, pointing to his tie tack. But Dunkle went even further. He promised that if Congress passed a bill forcing Yellowstone Park reintroduction, he'd use every bureaucratic means at his disposal to delay implementing the law. "If you've seen bureaucracy in action," he said, "you know the Glacier [Park] wolves are likely to reach Yellowstone before the paperwork is done."

A Casper *Star-Tribune* columnist described Dunkle's behavior before the woolgrowers this way: "If Dunkle were a wolf, he would have licked the woolgrowers' noses, rolled over on his back, and peed on himself. Any wolf would recognize that as submissive behavior."

The Wyoming delegation ruled. Mott was silenced. Dunkle was stalling. The livestock industry was enraged by the Browning incident. It was a low point for Yellowstone Park wolf advocates. Then, on the last day of September 1987, I got a startling call from a newspaper reporter. He wanted me to comment on legislation a congressman had introduced the day before that directed the secretary of the interior to reintroduce wolves to Yellowstone Park within the next three years.

I was floored. I had knocked on dozens of doors in Washington, D.C., but had never met anyone bold enough to introduce such legislation. Utah Representative Wayne Owens was the author of the bill. He'd taken a trip to Yellowstone Park for the House Interior Committee, which is responsible for national parks. There he learned how the Wyoming congressional delegation recently had squashed Mott and Yellowstone Park wolf restoration. "As I was sitting on the airplane, flying back to Washington, I began thinking, 'If they can stop it politically, maybe I can get it started again that way.'" Owens later told me. "And that's when I decided to introduce my legislation."

The members of the Wyoming congressional delegation weren't happy campers. This upstart congressman obviously didn't understand the rules of the game. "Let us worry about Wyoming," Cheney said in the Casper *Star-Tribune*. He sarcastically noted that maybe the Wyoming delegation would have to see about reintroducing sharks to Great Salt Lake. Owens replied with the refreshing naiveté of a relative newcomer to Congress: "Yellowstone Park does not belong to Wyoming. It belongs to all of us."

The most significant breakthroughs seem to happen amid the greatest adversity. Wayne Brewster was sitting in his Helena office (the Fish and Wildlife Service endangered species office had moved there from Billings in 1983) in November 1987, still picking up the pieces from the Browning disaster. In walked Frank Dunkle. Helena was Dunkle's hometown, so a visit from him wasn't altogether unusual. But Dunkle closed the door and told Brewster he wanted to talk about wolves.

Brewster braced for the worst, expecting a harsh reprimand for supporting wolf restoration. Instead, Dunkle, enigmatic as ever, asked, "If you were going to manage wolves properly in Montana, what would you do?"

Brewster had his response down cold. For more than a year, he'd been asking for money to hire experienced people and buy equipment to capture wolves, to no avail. He laid it out.

"How much would that cost?" Dunkle asked.

"About $200,000," Brewster replied, pointing out that he'd

already made the request several times.

"I'll tell you what," Dunkle said. "Why don't you try making that request one more time?" Brewster did, and soon he had money to buy equipment and create a Fish and Wildlife Service wolf team.

Why did Dunkle provide wolf recovery money? In his speeches, he often emphasized that the Fish and Wildlife Service had to solve livestock depredation problems in northwestern Montana before anyone could even think about reintroducing wolves to Yellowstone Park. Brewster theorizes that "delivering the funding may have been a way of proving up on his rhetoric."

Then again, perhaps the always-astute Dunkle read the political situation more clearly than others, including me. Establishing an effective Montana wolf recovery program did prove critical to winning acceptance for Yellowstone Park wolf reintroduction.

The summer from hell brought several positive outcomes. It forced Defenders to develop a compensation program. It also prompted Dunkle to find the money that resulted in the hiring of Ed Bangs, who eventually would guide the Fish and Wildlife Service's Yellowstone Park wolf restoration effort. And it provoked the first legislation requiring wolf reintroduction to the park.

Public support for wolf recovery remained strong despite the setbacks. The University of Montana's Bureau of Business and Economic Research—a conservative polling group supported mainly by business interests—conducted a statewide poll for the *Great Falls Tribune* on Montanans' attitudes toward wolves. Despite the Browning incident, nearly two-thirds of Montanans said they believed wolves belong in the state. In fact, most said wolves should be reintroduced to Montana, Idaho, and Yellowstone Park.

Maybe it hadn't been such a bad summer, after all.

T E N

WOLVES ARE FUN

A biologist with attitude: that's what Wayne Brewster got when he hired Ed Bangs in 1988 to lead the Fish and Wildlife Service's Montana wolf recovery program. Bangs brought to the job a happy irreverence and a snappy answer for every silly question. Full of energy and enthusiasm, Bangs *likes* high-profile controversies that put people in his face. He enjoys talking with irate ranchers and demanding hunters. He thrives on excitement and challenge.

Most state and federal agencies at the time treated wolves like a highly contagious disease that should be avoided if possible and apologized for if contracted. Correcting this agency defensiveness became Bangs's first mission. "Wolves are fun," he told everyone he talked with. "Have joy in your work!" Combat-hardened agency biologists looked at him as if he'd been air-freighted in from la-la land. Bangs didn't care; he had a "Wolves Are Fun!" T-shirt made up to emphasize his point.

"Why apologize for bringing back wolves?" he asked. "Wildlife agencies rightfully take great pride in the restoration of elk and bighorn sheep to their original ranges in the western United States. Why not take the same pride in restoring wolves? They're fascinating animals that deserve our attention."

Bangs's ardor inspired camaraderie and cooperation. He was like a puppy urging old dogs to play. He showed fellow workers that it could be exciting to work for a government wildlife agency. Bangs had a good joke or wisecrack for every occasion. As often as not, his target was himself or the Fish and Wildlife Service.

He thought that all agencies were too uptight about wolves' impacts on humans. "They don't attack people," he'd say. "They don't create land-use restrictions. They don't hurt the economy. They may eat livestock, but only a little. Besides, they're attractive, and most people like them and see them as a symbol of the wild." He urged the Forest Service, Park Service, and Fish and Wildlife Service to relax a little. "Wolves are no big deal" was a constant Bangs refrain.

Bangs didn't understand why people couldn't view wolves as they did mountain lions. "Montana has thousands of mountain lions," he'd point out. "They sometimes kill stock, they frequently kill deer and elk, and they even occasionally attack people. But no one in Montana is pushing to get rid of them." Westerners, who'd lived with mountain lions for decades, considered the big cats another part of the landscape. "When people see a mountain lion, they don't dash for their .30-30 with the idea of killing it," he said. For most people, a glimpse of a mountain lion provided a lifetime memory, well worth the occasional loss of a calf or a deer.

Extensive experience with people and wolves had prepared Bangs for the challenge he faced in the Northern Rockies. For thirteen years, he'd been a wildlife biologist at Alaska's Kenai National Wildlife Refuge. Hunters had eliminated wolves from the Kenai Peninsula in the early 1900s, but wolves started recolonizing the area in 1967. The number of wolves increased slowly at first but grew rapidly once the population had reached about fifty.

Rolf Peterson—one of the original Isle Royale researchers—studied the return of the Kenai wolves, and Bangs helped by capturing wolves and radio collaring them. Bangs participated in the capture of over eighty wolves, using leg-hold traps or shooting them with tranquilizer darts from a helicopter. Despite his long association with wolves, Bangs says he developed no special attachment to them. "Wild animals and wild spaces molded me into who I am and define my personal and professional life," he told me. "But wolves are no more important to me than any other species. I've never been particularly caught up in the whole magic of wolves. And I have no compunction about killing wolves if that's what's required to solve a problem, like wolves' killing livestock."

Controversy surrounded the Fish and Wildlife Service's wolf recovery program when Bangs took over. For a person who reveled in conflict, he was in hog heaven. Other state and federal agencies and the public didn't like or understand the Fish and Wildlife Service's wolf restoration plans. The agencies had no confidence that the Fish and Wildlife Service would control wolves if the animals caused problems, and some segments of the public feared major land-use restrictions.

The Fish and Wildlife Service and Montana's Department of Fish, Wildlife and Parks constantly squabbled in public over endangered species management. The Fish and Wildlife Service had other agency relationship problems as well. Since the Browning wolf fiasco, Fish and Wildlife Service and Animal Damage Control employees barely spoke to one another. The Fish and Wildlife Service's wolf recovery effort was a leaky boat.

Bangs's first order of business was to establish the Fish and Wildlife Service as a credible source of information on wolves. He developed a wolf recovery roadshow he took to Forest Service offices, Rotary Clubs, conservation groups, state wildlife offices, and almost any other place he could gather some people and plug in his slide projector. Between 1988 and 1992, Bangs and other Fish and Wildlife Service employees gave over three hundred presentations to nearly fourteen thousand people.

Bangs had an entertaining style and a knack for sizing up his audience. To conservation groups, he stressed the need to kill or relocate wolves that attacked livestock; to livestock groups, he emphasized the infrequency of wolf-livestock conflicts and ways to reduce the number even more.

One evening, Bangs found himself in Eureka, a small logging town in extreme northwestern Montana. His audience was the Tobacco Valley Rod and Gun Club, a local sportsmen's group. The word was out: the government guy was in town to talk about wolves.

Before the meeting started, a grizzled old local went to the front of the room and slapped a weather-beaten book down on the podium. It was a publication from the early 1900s, *How to Trap and Poison Wolves and Coyotes*. It could have been one of the early tomes of the Biological Survey's Vernon Bailey.

Bangs picked up the book and slowly paged through it, all the while murmuring quietly. "I've done that," he said. "This looks interesting. I don't think I've read this before." He was toying with the old-timer, just as the old-timer was toying with him.

"He was testing me," Bangs told me later. "He was saying, 'Screw with us, and we'll kill every wolf around.' They wanted to see if I was a tree-hugger who would start bawling if they said they were going to kill wolves. I told them I had killed plenty of wolves and that it was no big deal. I also reminded them there was a big fine for killing wolves and I hoped they wouldn't do it."

Bangs brought that same matter-of-factness about wolves to meetings of government land and wildlife managers. Eyebrows raised when he invited John Gunson, carnivore biologist for Alberta's provincial fish and wildlife agency, to meet with Montana state and federal officials. Gunson had a reputation as a law-and-order wolf man. Alberta has a substantial wolf population, but the Canadians have never been shy about killing wolves. Gunson urged wolf restoration in Montana. But he stressed that winning wolf support from the livestock industry and sportsmen would require a rational policy implemented with consistency and integrity. Bangs scored major points with state officials for inviting a person with such a practical viewpoint.

The conflict between the Fish and Wildlife Service and Montana's Department of Fish, Wildlife and Parks ran much deeper than wolves. State officials had been feuding with the Fish and Wildlife Service over endangered species ever since the agency had listed the grizzly bear in 1975. Black-footed ferret recovery provided another source of friction. In fact, the state had a chip on its shoulder. Almost all endangered species issues degenerated into turf battles over the state's right to manage its wildlife.

State agencies normally manage all wildlife species except migratory birds. Because ducks and geese migrate across state and national borders, states have been willing to concede that federal management makes sense. State wildlife agencies, however, remain closely involved with managing even those species. The Endangered Species Act of 1973 changed this dynamic. It gave the federal Fish and Wildlife Service primary responsibility for threatened and endangered species. When Congress was considering the legislation, almost all states opposed this change. Western states led the resistance, and Montana was among the most vociferous.

The Montana state-federal relationship reached its low point only a few months after Bangs's arrival. Montana Fish, Wildlife and Parks Director K. L. Cool became so angry during an endangered species meeting that he literally kicked Kemper McMaster, the Fish and Wildlife Service's Montana office supervisor, out of his office.

Bangs took a different approach. He realized that he couldn't influence high-level people like Cool, who respond mostly to political pressures. Instead, Bangs focused on informing state wildlife agency employees who lived and worked near the communities where wolf recovery was happening. Bangs recognized that game wardens, biologists, information officers, secretaries, and maintenance people could be important local opinion leaders. So, although Montana maintained an official position of noninvolvement with wolf recovery throughout the late 1980s, many state employees played important unofficial roles.

Bangs went beyond the informational approach and took direct action to mend fences with Animal Damage Control. He invited representatives of the predator-control agency to wolf meetings and sought their advice on the final version of the Fish and Wildlife Service's wolf control plan. Most often, he spoke with Carter Niemeyer, Animal Damage Control's Helena district supervisor.

Niemeyer is an Animal Damage Control anomaly. Although most of his agency's trappers have extensive field experience but little formal education, Niemeyer has both. He earned a master's degree in wildlife management and has been trapping since age nine. Highly respected within his agency, Niemeyer has a reputation as a reformer. Although he frequently exhorts Animal Damage Control to be more professional and scientific, when scratched, he bleeds "Type ADC" blood.

Like soldiers, Bangs and Niemeyer cemented their relationship in battle. In the fall of 1989, Bangs received his first crisis alert. Wolves had killed a calf near the small town of Marion, not far from Kalispell. Within a day, Bangs and Niemeyer were on the scene.

They made an effective team. Niemeyer knew many of the ranchers in western Montana. Even though most stockmen inherently dislike the federal government, they respected Niemeyer's honesty and candor. So, the ranchers gave Bangs a chance as well. His friendliness soon won them over.

Bangs knew how to catch wolves. Niemeyer, who knew how to catch everything else, learned quickly. Bangs also brought an important wolf-catching technique from Alaska to the northern Rockies: tranquilizer darts and helicopters. Once biologists had radio collared a wolf, they usually could locate the pack and capture the animals. Helicopters were expensive, but air power might have resolved the Browning incident in a few days. At Marion, Bangs and Niemeyer, helped by other Fish and Wildlife Service biologists, caught four wolves—two adults and two pups—and relocated them to Glacier Park.

The problems stopped for a while. Three of the wolves died

soon thereafter, but the fourth—an adult female—survived and eventually produced a litter of pups in the Nine Mile area, about twenty miles west of Missoula.

The remaining Marion wolves began attacking livestock again the following spring, killing several calves. The incident generated the same intensive press coverage and wolf hysteria the Browning affair had 2½ years earlier. Media interest soared when an animal rights organization called the Wolf Action Group appeared on the scene and began interfering with Fish and Wildlife Service trapping efforts. Group members, opposed to all wolf-killing, walked along Bangs and Niemeyer's trap lines in hopes of saving a wolf.

Ironically, the group's actions may have had the opposite effect. Bangs had planned to trap any remaining wolves, fit them with radio collars, and release them in Glacier Park. But when trapping failed—partly because of the activists' interference and partly because of bad weather—Bangs told Niemeyer to dart the next wolf if possible and kill it if necessary. Unable to maneuver a helicopter close enough to shoot a dart, Niemeyer killed a wolf. That put an end to the stock-killing.

After the successful experiment of compensating the Browning ranchers, Defenders of Wildlife's board of directors had authorized the creation of a permanent Wolf Compensation Fund, with a funding goal of $100,000. Defenders paid the four Marion ranchers who'd lost livestock a total of about $5,500—market value—for the loss of two cows and thirteen calves. Again, compensation seemed to douse the fire.

The Marion incident had a better conclusion than the Browning episode. When Bangs and Niemeyer left, local ranchers were satisfied; their problem had been corrected, their livestock losses covered. None told the newspapers that in the future, they'd shoot wolves on sight. Few complained about the Fish and Wildlife Service or Animal Damage Control. And no one questioned whether the Fish and Wildlife Service would swiftly remedy any wolf attacks on livestock that might occur later.

The control action also boosted the survival chances of the growing number of other wolf packs in Montana—packs that weren't killing livestock. Fish and Wildlife Service data showed that, despite occasional wolf deaths, the state's wolf population was increasing a little more than 20 percent a year. The Fish and Wildlife Service finally had a credible program in place, and there were results to show for it.

Although the Fish and Wildlife Service was solving some complex wolf problems, the wolf wars raged on. Tom France and I had gained an important new ally. Renée Askins—who'd been involved with the wolf recovery team and the *Wolves and Humans* exhibit—had returned to Wyoming from Yale University, where she'd earned a master's degree in wildlife ecology. In 1990, she officially founded The Wolf Fund, a conservation group with a single mission: restoring wolves to Yellowstone Park. She soon started a regional lecture series and a national media campaign.

Wolves were already in the news, of course. Extremist groups on both ends of the spectrum kept the feuds going, and the media couldn't get enough of the controversy. Environmentalists versus ranchers: it was a modern version of frontier-day "entertainment," when westerners put a bear and a bison in the same arena just for the thrill of watching them fight.

The extremist Wolf Action Group, led by John Lilburn, was a rancher's worst nightmare. Its members weren't just pro-wolf; they also hated cows and wanted to rid public lands of them. Some ranchers even considered the members dangerous. The Wolf Action Group was a spinoff of Earth First!, a radical environmental group that condones what it calls "eco-sabotage" in defense of the environment.

As Sir Isaac Newton said, for every action there's an opposite and equal reaction. The flip side of John Lilburn's Wolf Action Group was Troy Mader's Abundant Wildlife Society, a virulent anti-wolf organization. Mader based his opposition to wolves not on science but on "history." A pamphlet entitled *12 Historically Proven Facts About Wolves* included such amazing insights as "Wolves are cruel—

they eat their prey alive and leave them to suffer" and "Wolves kill everything." My personal favorite is "Wolves desecrated the graves of early settlers." The wolves couldn't do anything right. One of the Abundant Wildlife Society's pet sayings was "Wolves Are Nature's Criminals."

Mader grew up near Gillette, Wyoming, where his ultraconservative family ran a religious radio station. One of his first crusades was against homosexuals and the spread of AIDS. After a short stint in law enforcement, Mader found his true calling: opposing wolf restoration.

Despite their high media visibility, it was hard to take the Wolf Action Group and the Abundant Wildlife Society too seriously. One was an out-of-control bunch of brat-pack college students, the other a right-wing zealot in need of something to hate. Both defined themselves by what they opposed, not what they supported. Neither represented anyone but itself.

One night, on a drive home from yet another wolf meeting, Pat Tucker, the National Wildlife Federation's wolf specialist in the northern Rockies, and I had a flash of insight about wolf extremists. "Have you ever considered that the Montana Stockgrowers Association might be doing something incredibly clever?" I asked.

"No," she said. That thought had never crossed her mind.

"What if the stockgrowers hired John Lilburn and instructed him to wear funny clothes and let his hair grow long?" I wondered aloud. "Then what if they told him to trespass on ranchers' land, interfere with government biologists, stick a few 'Wolves Not Cows' bumper stickers on ranchers' pickups, and be as rabid as possible? Everyone would think that environmentalists are selfish and hate people. Then no one would support wolf recovery."

She caught my drift and smiled.

"But we'd outsmart them," Tucker said. "We'd scour small-town Wyoming until we found the right man. We'd tell him to act as if he'd been born a hundred years ago, that slaughtering the buffalo and trapping out the beaver were good things." She was getting into this now.

"We'd forbid him to read anything factual," she continued. "We'd make him go to small towns to give anti-wolf speeches based on bar talk and gossip. People would conclude that ranchers are selfish and hate wildlife. Then everyone would support wolves."

We laughed all the way back to Missoula.

ELEVEN

IN THE PUZZLE PALACE

Now that Fish and Wildlife Service brass finally had signed the recovery plan, conservationists had a new goal: to compel the government agencies to start a Yellowstone Park wolf environmental impact statement, EIS for short. It wasn't that we enjoyed reading thick, arcane government documents or attending boring, bureaucratic public meetings. But several environmental groups had held meetings over the winter and agreed that an EIS was an inevitable, beneficial, and legally required precursor to bringing wolves back to the park.

The National Environmental Policy Act, passed by Congress in 1969 and enacted in 1970, requires federal agencies to prepare an environmental impact statement when undertaking something that will significantly affect people or the environment; restoring populations of large predators certainly falls into that category. More than a document, an EIS is a lengthy process aimed at getting the public involved in governmental decisions before they're made. It works like this: An agency drafts a document describing its proposal and alternative ways to achieve a goal. Then the agency distributes its draft and encourages public comment. Finally, the issues people raise in their comments are addressed by the agency and incorporated into a final EIS. The process is designed to ensure that government officials adequately consider all relevant facts and concerns before making important decisions.

Federal agencies don't need congressional approval to undertake environmental impact statements. In fact, Congress, which avoids micro-management, rarely starts them. Congress normally grants agencies almost complete discretion to decide whether or when to initiate environmental impact statements.

The Yellowstone Park wolf EIS was a special case because the Wyoming congressional delegation had forced the Reagan administration—and, later, Bush's—to agree *not* to start an EIS. The only way conservationists could steer around the roadblock was to persuade Congress to disregard the Wyoming politicians' wishes. Two possible routes existed. The simpler, more direct path was to have Congress appropriate money to produce a Yellowstone Park wolf EIS. The alternative was to have Congress pass legislation directing the Park Service or Fish and Wildlife Service to start an EIS. Legislation not involving appropriations goes through a much more protracted process, creating many opportunities for failure.

It was a formidable challenge. In the spring of 1988, I dusted off my suit and headed for the Puzzle Palace—a fellow lobbyist's code word for Washington's Capitol Hill. Dozens of visits to many congressional offices by many conservationists had considerably whittled down the list of prospective wolf supporters. We knew the lay of the land—whom to court and whom to avoid. My first stop was Idaho Senator Jim McClure.

I was apprehensive as I walked up to McClure's third-floor suite in the Hart Senate Office Building. Some environmental colleagues had openly criticized Defenders of Wildlife and the National Wildlife Federation for forging a working relationship with McClure aide Carl Haywood. A regional Sierra Club representative I respected had lectured me recently, "Don't ever forget: At the most fundamental level, McClure is not our friend. He doesn't need, nor does he seek, our votes to get elected. He does not want to please us or make us happy. We should not have Senator McClure be our champion on wolves or any other issue. It gives me the feeling of being on a stage-coach filled with payroll money without my shotgun."

He viewed talking to McClure as akin to sleeping with the enemy. At the same time, he and other conservationists acknowledged that McClure's solid support for wolf restoration had tempered the shrill rhetoric of the Wyoming congressional delegation. McClure's power and influence also made it politically safer for Park Service and Fish and Wildlife Service employees to work toward bringing wolves back to Yellowstone Park and central Idaho. Anyone assessing the political landscape—even the Wyoming Republicans—knew that McClure was the region's alpha member of Congress.

Carl Haywood, who'd set up the spring 1988 meeting, greeted Rupert Cutler and me in the senator's outer office. Cutler, who was then the president of Defenders, had been assistant secretary of agriculture in charge of the Forest Service during the Carter admin-istration. He knew McClure well; they'd frequently butted heads over wilderness and national forest management issues.

Haywood ushered us into McClure's office, where the four of us began making small talk. McClure told us he was deeply interested in the outdoors and enjoyed bird-watching. "Most of us who live in Idaho know that we can make more money by going somewhere else," he said, "but we live in Idaho by choice because of our outdoor lifestyle."

He seemed sincere enough. McClure wasn't the fire-breathing, Darth Vader-like politician I'd been prepared to meet. He was a real gentleman. Exceedingly polite, he listened as much as he talked. The soft-spoken, attentive McClure seemed every bit the country lawyer his biography in the *Congressional Directory* said he'd been before entering politics. He also was a busy man, so we cut the banter short.

I told McClure we appreciated his support for wolf recovery in central Idaho and Yellowstone Park but were frustrated that other western members of Congress continued delaying progress in restoring wolves. I asked him what he thought Defenders should do to advance the issue.

He'd already thought this through. "We must try to limit the recovery effort to places where there is the least conflict between man and animal," he said. "And we must aggressively manage conflict that occurs outside the primary recovery zone." We had no problems with anything he'd said so far.

He explained further, "That means that we select recovery areas like Glacier Park, Yellowstone Park, and the central Idaho wilderness areas, where there is no grazing and, therefore, little chance of direct conflict." I was impressed that he had such a good grasp of the issue.

He expressed concern that livestock losses near Browning the previous year had taken so long to resolve. "If we expect the ranchers near Yellowstone Park to accept wolf reintroduction, they must know that if wolves come outside the park and start causing problems, the rancher will be able to protect his livestock." He complimented Defenders for compensating the Browning stockmen.

McClure hadn't presented any insurmountable obstacles. We told him we thought that all his wolf restoration concerns could be accommodated by the experimental population provision of the Endangered Species Act. That clause would let people in the region customize their wolf restoration plan. The best way to develop such a plan, we suggested, was through an environmental impact statement. We told him the Park Service estimated that it would require a $200,000 appropriation to start a Yellowstone Park wolf EIS in 1989.

McClure was noncommittal. Although he supported the concept of the Endangered Species Act, he had problems with the way some people used it. "I'm concerned that the law has become a tool for people who wish to accomplish things other than just preserving endangered species," he said.

He cited the snail darter issue in Tennessee. Conservationists had raised legitimate concerns about building the Tellico Dam on the Tennessee River, he conceded. Prime farmland along the river bottom would have been lost, and the economic benefits of the project were questionable. But when conservationists didn't prevail on those issues, they made the snail darter the issue. "The snail darter was not unique to that site—they've since been found in a number of other places," he said. McClure worried that environmentalists in the northern Rockies similarly would use the wolf to pursue other agendas.

He handed Cutler and me a copy of a two-page wolf reintroduction proposal. He asked us to take it with us, look it over, and get back to him.

Before leaving, I asked McClure one final question: "I have to be honest with you. Many of our conservation allies don't view you as a friend. They want to know why you've become so involved with the wolf issue. What's your real motive?" I hoped I hadn't offended him.

He smiled knowingly and replied, "There's a balance that needs to be struck, and polarization will not produce the solutions. That's really what I'm trying to do—find a solution for an issue that's become so polarized there's no forward motion."

I knew his answer wouldn't satisfy my skeptical friends, but the meeting had been useful. No other member of Congress in the three-state area, Democrat or Republican, was even willing to say that wolves belonged anywhere in the northern Rockies. The government's leading wildlife official—Fish and Wildlife Service Director Frank Dunkle— had vowed to sabotage reintroducing wolves to Yellowstone Park. By contrast, McClure had handed us a concrete proposal for reintroducing wolves to Yellowstone Park *and* central Idaho. This was a milestone. Conservationists had envisioned natural recolonization of Idaho by wolves; we'd never proposed reintroducing wolves there as in Yellowstone Park. McClure was out in front of us on that.

McClure's proposal, however, had several fatal flaws. Most objectionable was a requirement that Congress remove the wolf from the endangered species list *before* reintroduction could occur. This unprecedented action would repudiate the important, carefully designed process for endangered species recovery that had been in place for fifteen years. I knew that conservationists would never agree to subvert a law as important to wildlife conservation as the Endangered Species Act. But McClure at least was holding open a door that might lead to a plan that *was* acceptable. We no longer were engaging in the mind-numbing debate over *whether* wolves belonged in the Northern Rockies; now we were debating *how* to restore the species. Wolf restoration had crossed an important threshold, although it proved difficult for some conservationists to see that change as progress.

Cutler and I visited Utah Representative Wayne Owens next. Owens had introduced the bill the previous fall mandating Yellowstone Park wolf reintroduction. Owens was knowledgeable about wolves and full of enthusiasm. He'd read several wolf books and recently learned about the complexities of wolf management while spending time with Dave Mech in Minnesota. Mech had told me Owens was one of the most inquisitive people he'd ever met. I liked the congressman. He was articulate, practical, and determined.

Owens acknowledged that he'd introduced his 1987 bill solely to alert the Wyoming congressional delegation to the strong national interest in Yellowstone Park wolf restoration. His next bill would be more substantive, he said. We talked strategy. Cutler and I suggested that if legislation proved necessary, most conservationists would favor a bill simply directing the Park Service to prepare a Yellowstone Park wolf EIS within a certain time period. We were sure that a fair, open-ended process would convince people that wolves belong in the park. So, there was no need for special legislation mandating wolf reintroduction. After all, that was precisely our objection to Senator McClure's proposal: it dictated a particular course of action, circumventing existing laws—namely, the National Environmental Policy Act and the Endangered Species Act. We thought that these laws, given a fair chance, could put all McClure's concerns to rest. Owens agreed.

Next, Cutler and I visited Neal Sigmon, an aide to Illinois

Democratic Representative Sidney Yates, chairman of the House Interior Appropriations Subcommittee. Sigmon's modest title of "clerk" belied his influence; he had more influence over the budgets of the Park Service and Fish and Wildlife Service than did almost anyone else in the country. He assembled budget requests and set priorities for the committee's consideration.

Sigmon was inscrutable. As I gave my pitch, I couldn't tell whether he knew or cared about restoring wolves to Yellowstone Park. He didn't appear distracted; he listened attentively, took notes, and occasionally asked good questions. He just didn't give anything away. When I pressed him on the likelihood of a $200,000 appropriation for a Yellowstone Park wolf EIS, he gave a guarded reply. The only positive note came at the end of the meeting, when he told me he appreciated hearing from people outside Washington's Beltway. I took it as encouragement. His parting advice was to get House members—particularly those on the Interior Appropriations Subcommittee—to write letters to Yates requesting the $200,000.

We did just that, placing several letters on Yates's desk. In June 1988, the House passed an appropriations bill that included $200,000 to start a Yellowstone Park wolf EIS. Conservationists were ecstatic.

What followed became a fall ritual reminiscent of the annual "Peanuts" comic strip in which Lucy tees up a football for Charlie Brown to kick, only to pull it away at the last second.

The Senate version of the appropriations bill contained no Yellowstone Park wolf EIS money. When House and Senate versions of legislation don't agree, a conference committee composed of some members of each body hammers out compromises. The horse-trading by the conference committee on appropriations can be intense; dams and interpretive centers may get swapped for fish hatcheries and additions to wildlife refuges.

Although the Wyoming congressional delegation strenuously opposed funding a Yellowstone Park wolf EIS, none of its members was on the Appropriations Committee, so their influence was limited. McClure, the committee's ranking Republican, held all the cards.

McClure responded to the Wyoming politicians' concerns with a compromise forged with House Subcommittee Chairman Yates: Congress wouldn't fund an EIS but would appropriate $200,000 for the Park Service and Fish and Wildlife Service to study potential effects of Yellowstone Park wolf reintroduction on big-game animals, grizzly bears, livestock, and the local economy. These studies became known by their collective title, *Wolves for Yellowstone?* Accompanying the bill was a committee report that detailed congressional intent. In it, the committee members declared, "The return of the wolf to Yellowstone Park is desirable."

Key Park Service and Fish and Wildlife Service officials were delighted. The report plainly showed Congressional support for Yellowstone Park wolf restoration, and the language could be used as a shield to repel the sharp spears of the Wyoming politicians. Some agency officials viewed initiating the congressional wolf studies as equivalent to starting an EIS.

Conservationists weren't nearly as happy. The victory seemed more philosophical than substantive. Most wolf advocates viewed the approach as a classic congressional stalling tactic: instead of doing something, study it. Wolves already were one of the most-studied animals in North America. Did Congress really need to spend $200,000 to develop site-specific information on how wolves might affect Yellowstone Park? I didn't think so.

The controversy over Yellowstone Park wolf restoration centered on values, not science. As western historian J. Frank Dobie once observed, "Putting on the spectacles of science in expectation of finding the answer to everything signifies inner blindness." If you peeled away the layers of this onion, the core issue was clear: were people willing to share the land with a fellow predator? At one extreme, people said that human needs must come first. At the other, people held that wolves should come first. Science alone wouldn't help us find the middle ground. The solution inevitably would be political.

What happened the following year was like going to a bad movie twice. Congressman Owens introduced a bill in May 1989 directing the Park Service to complete a Yellowstone Park wolf EIS within two years. The legislation became an important vehicle for rallying support and creating visibility for wolf restoration.

Timm Kaminski—the wildlife biologist who'd worked closely with the wolf recovery team in the early 1980s and researched the status of wolves in central Idaho—now was Owens's legislative assistant and a valuable source of information for conservationists, resource agencies, and other congressional staffers. He continually bolstered efforts to secure wolf funds and helped arrange opportunities for Owens to keep Yellowstone Park wolf restoration in the public spotlight. One notable success was Owens's appearance on national television with a live wolf on the steps of the Capitol. Owens and conservationists realized that getting the House to pass his bill was a long shot; getting the Senate to enact it was "Mission Impossible." In the end, the House held a hearing, but the bill failed to advance.

McClure, meanwhile, continued to circulate and refine his wolf reintroduction proposal. The plan gained credibility when biologist Dave Mech gave it his stamp of approval. Haywood had been doing his homework. Mech believed that if a small wolf population became established through reintroduction—as provided under the McClure bill—wolf numbers would continue to increase with no special changes in land management. He was confident that existing national parks and wilderness areas would provide enough refuge for wolves, so they wouldn't need much additional protection to prosper.

Tom France of the National Wildlife Federation told Haywood that McClure's proposal had no future unless the senator could bring the livestock industry to the negotiating table. On several occasions, Haywood tried to do so but never could enlist more than a few Idaho stockmen. The industry, led by the Wyoming Farm Bureau, refused to back away from its "No wolves, no way" stance.

At the end of 1989, the House of Representatives voted to appropriate money for a Yellowstone Park wolf EIS, but McClure snatched the funds away again. Congress instead appropriated $175,000 for more studies on the effects of wolf reintroduction but expressly forbade agencies to prepare an EIS.

Then came big news. In 1990, McClure announced that he intended to retire at the end of the year. One of his final legislative priorities would be passing his Yellowstone Park and Idaho wolf reintroduction proposal. In May, he introduced a bill aimed at accomplishing wolf restoration.

Conservationists debated whether even McClure—at this point a lame duck—had the connections to get the bill passed. We all were aware of his talent for last-minute legislating, but there was relatively little time left. Even innocuous bills can take months or years to make it to the president's desk.

The first two volumes of the *Wolves for Yellowstone?* studies also came out in May 1990. They held few surprises for the informed. Scientists concluded that Yellowstone Park wolf restoration would have a minimal effect on the livestock industry; grizzly bears; the area's seven species of ungulates (large grazing mammals); or the economies of communities surrounding the park. In fact, the authors of the report predicted that people's great interest in wolves would cause local economies to benefit substantially from increased tourism. Although the report's conclusions may not have been earth-shattering, the *Wolves for Yellowstone?* studies played an essential role in public education and laid the foundation for a rock-solid EIS.

The big showdown came in September, when McClure called a hearing before the Senate Subcommittee on Public Lands, National Parks and Forests. If McClure could build enough support at the hearing, he'd no doubt try to add his wolf bill to another piece of legislation and muscle it through Congress in the waning moments of the session.

The hearing included testimony from the usual players: ranchers; bureaucrats; congressional opponents; and conservationists (Tom France, Greater Yellowstone Coalition President Tom McNamee, and me). But it produced a couple of major surprises. The first came from a panel representing the Park Service, Forest Service, and Fish and Wildlife Service. The heads of those agencies had huddled before the McClure hearing and agreed on their testimony: they wouldn't support the McClure bill but would endorse Yellowstone Park wolf reintroduction. In the federal bureaucracy, developing such a position involves much more than writing testimony and presenting it at a hearing. If congressional testimony contains significant policy implications, agencies must obtain approval from a high-ranking departmental official or the appropriate cabinet secretary and then run an advance copy by the Office of Management and Budget. If OMB approves it, the testimony becomes the official administration position. A few brave bureaucrats had advocated returning wolves to Yellowstone Park—most notably, Bill Mott, whom President Bush hadn't reappointed after taking office in 1989. But President Reagan's administration had never taken a formal stand on wolf reintroduction, nor had that of Bush. Until now.

OMB cleared the agencies' testimony on the McClure bill, including endorsement of the goal of wolf restoration. Federal agencies at last were out in the open. Yellowstone Park wolf reintroduction now was official Bush administration policy.

An even bigger surprise was to come. The final witnesses who appeared that day were representatives of the livestock industry, including the American Farm Bureau Federation, Wyoming Wool Growers Association, Idaho Wool Growers Association, and Montana Stockgrowers Association. Most stridently opposed McClure's bill. Only the Idaho Wool Growers, one of the West's more progressive livestock organizations, offered lukewarm endorsement. The complaints were the same as always: predictions of rampant livestock depredation and onerous restrictions on land use. After the last livestock industry witness had finished, McClure looked tired and impatient. He hadn't generated support for his legislation. It frustrated him that the agricultural groups didn't see what he did—that wolf recovery was going to happen whether they liked it or not.

McClure said to the stockmen, "The thing I guess I am troubled with is you have outlined fears and concerns that you have about what may happen under my bill. None of you has really addressed what happens if there is no bill." He pointed out that wolves had returned to Montana on their own and could return similarly to Idaho and Yellowstone Park.

Wyoming Senator Malcolm Wallop jumped into the proceeding. "I have to say what Jim McClure has done is to point out a reality," he declared. "The reality is that recovery, one way or another, is going to take place. It is either longer and natural or shorter and controlled. . . . It is not fair to the people you represent to pretend that it is never going to take place."

I couldn't believe my ears. I nudged France, who was sitting next to me. We looked over at John Varley of the Park Service. His mouth was agape. Wallop was telling the livestock industry to get with the program. *Wallop*, of all people! Could success be far away?

Farther than we thought, it turned out. The McClure bill died. Meanwhile, the House had again passed an appropriations bill containing money for a Yellowstone Park wolf EIS, and McClure once more had blocked it in the Senate. But he was intent on forcing the livestock industry to accept the reality of wolf recovery. He believed that stockmen needed to participate in wolf reintroduction in order to have some say in how it was administered. He didn't trust the resource agencies to look out for livestock interests. McClure helped bring about a conference report directing the secretary of the interior to appoint a ten-person Wolf Management Committee. Congress appropriated $375,000 for the group to develop a wolf reintroduction and management plan for Yellowstone Park and central Idaho. The committee would be made up of agency leaders and members of the public, including livestock industry and conservation group representatives. The group had until May 15, 1991, to submit a report to Congress.

McClure retired from the Senate as planned, unable to break the impasse over wolf restoration. Conservationists still argue over whether he wanted to atone for his dismal environmental record or was simply out to cut a better deal for his livestock industry friends. His motives don't matter. Intentionally or not, he breathed life into a cause that otherwise would have been dead on arrival on Capitol Hill.

The Wolf Management Committee became McClure's legacy—one last chance, it seemed, to resolve the issue of restoring wolves to Yellowstone Park and central Idaho through a meeting of the minds.

TWELVE

THE PERILS OF EXTREMISM

When the Wolf Management Committee began its negotiations on January 23, 1991, many conservationists thought the livestock industry's resistance to wolf reintroduction finally might be weakening. After all, the Yellowstone Park wolf debate had been dragging on for nearly a decade. Newspaper articles, national magazine features, and television specials had cranked wolves' public visibility so high that everyone knew that the issue wasn't going away. Many people—even some livestock leaders—now considered Yellowstone Park wolf restoration inevitable.

Wolf numbers had continued to increase in Montana. Some livestock leaders ruminated on Senator McClure's logic: wouldn't it be smarter to make rules about wolf management *before* wolves arrived? Otherwise, there would be no bargaining. Once wolves moved in on their own, environmentalists would demand all the protection the Endangered Species Act affords.

What conservationists didn't know was that, shortly before McClure's Senate hearing, something had happened that had made livestock industry representatives anything but amenable to wolf restoration.

Jerry Jack, executive vice president of the Montana Stockgrowers Association, was one of the livestock industry leaders who listened thoughtfully to McClure's proposal when the senator first floated it in 1988. The debate over wolves frustrated him. Although wolf recovery affected only a small part of his membership, the continual uproar this issue created regularly diverted his attention from what he believed to be more critical concerns for ranchers: developing foreign markets for livestock, protecting water rights, and controlling access to public lands.

Each spring, the Montana Stockgrowers sent a delegation to Washington, D.C., to work on legislative matters. The delegates usually included the group's president, executive vice president, and several board members. Late one afternoon in April 1990, Jack and several Stockgrowers officers and board members visited Representative Ron Marlenee, the Montana Republican.

The Stockgrowers and Marlenee enjoyed a close relationship. As the livestock lobbyists sometimes remarked to one another, "He may be a son of a bitch, but he's our son of a bitch." Marlenee always voted their way. This afternoon, he was pouring them drinks, laughing, and telling stories.

As Jack recalls it, Marlenee kept a wolf pelt in his office that someone from Alaska had given him. He liked to show it off. Marlenee picked it up with a flourish and declared, "This is a 'good' wolf." And off they went, carping about wolves. Jack simmered; he'd been down this road before. Marlenee never wanted to talk about anything *but* wolves.

Finally, Jack spoke up. "Ron," he said, "I feel like an idiot telling people in Montana we can't live with wolves when we already have fifty or sixty in the state and nothing is going terribly wrong. When livestock losses occur, the agencies control the wolves and the ranchers can get compensation. And what if a pair of wolves makes it to Yellowstone on their own—where are we then? Here's my question:

what's the long-term solution to the wolf issue?"

Jack says the congressman blustered but offered no substantive response. "Marlenee was using the Stockgrowers as his hammer," Jack said. "He used the Stockgrowers to keep the issue brewing because he saw it as politically advantageous to do so. I didn't like it because we needed a solution."

At the Stockgrowers' summer 1990 convention, Jack decided to see whether the membership would change its "No wolves, no way" position. With the help of several board members and ranchers, Jack drafted a resolution—a watered-down version of the McClure proposal—that offered many safeguards for ranchers if federal agencies were to reintroduce wolves to Yellowstone Park.

Many rabid wolf-haters were in the audience of three hundred to four hundred ranchers, and they launched into spirited debate. But Jack remembers that, after three readings and a few changes, the membership supported the resolution. It was a milestone for the Montana Stockgrowers, an organization born a century earlier out of hatred for wolves.

But it was a short-lived milestone. A few weeks later, Congressman Marlenee began calling Stockgrowers board members to demand that they rescind the resolution. Moderating their position had made him look bad, he complained. The resolution had to be fixed. Reversing the group's position was tricky because its bylaws give only the full membership the right to pass or rescind resolutions. According to Jack, the group's new board and new president—a close friend of Marlenee's named Jim Courtney—skirted that policy and changed the resolution to suit the congressman.

"I was shocked," Jack told me later. "It was like holding an election and then disregarding the results. I have a value system that says you do what's right for the resources and the land. This was wrong."

But the resolution accommodating wolves wasn't the only thing Marlenee wanted changed. In August, the Stockgrowers fired Jack.

"Once the resolution passed and the officers rescinded it,

someone had to go," Jack said. "They couldn't fire the ranchers who voted for it. So, I had to walk the plank." In an interview with the Helena *Independent Record,* Courtney confirmed Marlenee's involvement in Jack's firing, acknowledging that the two "haven't gotten along in quite a while."

Jack's ousting sent a warning to other livestock industry leaders who might have been considering breaking ranks. It may help account for the ranchers' strong opposition to the McClure bill at the congressional hearing that came a few weeks later. It certainly hardened opposition to any compromise. In the livestock industry camp, anti-wolf extremists ruled.

In December, Secretary of the Interior Manuel Lujan, Jr., named ten people to the Wolf Management Committee: the directors of the state wildlife agencies of Montana, Idaho, and Wyoming; the regional forester of the Northern Region of the Forest Service and regional directors of the Park Service and Fish and Wildlife Service; and one representative for sportsmen's groups, one for the livestock industry, and two for conservation groups. Lujan chose Tom Dougherty, director of the National Wildlife Federation's Rocky Mountain office in Boulder, Colorado, and me as the conservation representatives.

The ink had barely dried on the Interior Department news release announcing the committee selection when Congressman Marlenee launched a frontal assault on Secretary Lujan. "The committee has been stacked with a predetermined bias to reintroduce the wolf," he charged. "The secretary [of the interior] himself has been sold down the river. The environmental activists have eaten his lunch."

Marlenee said that if Hollywood were to make a movie of the secretary's selection process, it would be called *Dunces with Wolves.*

In fact, only a person with Senator McClure's political acumen could have constructed a team so evenly balanced. After the first meeting in January 1991, it was clear that the committee was perfectly divided, five to five. Representatives of the federal agencies and conservation groups were on one side, supporting reintroduction of wolves to Yellowstone Park as an experimental population. Representatives of the state wildlife agencies and the livestock industry opposed reintroducing wolves, as did the representative of sportsmen's groups. Sportsmen actually got stiffed on the committee; the person appointed to represent hunters was the paid representative of the Idaho Cattle Association. The opponents' interests were diverse, but the group formed a united front against wolf recovery.

Surprisingly, the livestock industry wasn't the main impediment to a reasonable discussion of how to restore wolves to Yellowstone Park and central Idaho. That distinction went to K. L. Cool, the hotheaded, theatrical director of Montana's Department of Fish, Wildlife and Parks. He wasted no time in manipulating the Wolf Management Committee. His style reminded me of Frank Dunkle's: politics first, biology a distant second. Like Dunkle, Cool was politically adept. One moment, he was a bully. The next, he was submissive, almost servile.

Cool quickly assessed the makeup of the committee and organized the state agencies and the livestock industry to operate as a bloc of five votes. By doing so—and establishing himself as the leader—he claimed power to stop any proposal he didn't like. During every coffee break and at each critical juncture of a meeting, Cool huddled with the livestock industry and other state agency directors. He rarely spoke with the rest of us.

At the first meeting, Cool demanded that future management of Montana's existing wolf population be part of the Wolf Management Committee's recommendation. Several committee members protested, pointing out that Congress's charge to the committee was to develop a wolf reintroduction and management plan for Yellowstone Park and central Idaho—not Montana. Besides, wolf recovery was going smoothly in Montana.

Cool wouldn't relent, and the livestock industry-state agency cabal supported him. The Montana wolf management issue stayed on the table. Cool's group offered its proposal: Congress should remove wolves from the federal endangered species list in Montana, Idaho, and Wyoming—except in national parks and national wildlife refuges—before reintroducing wolves to Yellowstone Park. The proposal said that those states would assume sole responsibility for managing wolves. Private landowners would have broad discretion to kill wolves.

The federal agency heads, Tom Dougherty, and I knew that such a proposal could never win congressional approval. This approach was far more radical than McClure's, which had won no support. The proposal was nothing more than a clever way to say no to Yellowstone Park wolf reintroduction.

Cool and the gang, however, wouldn't budge. Tom Dougherty and I had long private conversations with the other state wildlife agency directors: Pete Petera of Wyoming and Jerry Conley of Idaho. They weren't enthusiastic about the ground Cool had staked out, but neither would change his position.

I'd known Conley for many years and respected his integrity and commitment to solving difficult problems. He was honest with me. "It would be political suicide for me to take a wolf recovery position different from Montana's or Wyoming's," he said. "If I did, our legislature would change it immediately. All three states must agree on any solution that comes out of this committee; that's a political reality." It was a political reality Cool understood all too well.

Conley and Petera had shown interest in the proposal advanced by the representatives of the federal agencies and conservation groups. We supported reintroducing wolves to Yellowstone Park as an experimental population and proposed a three-year study of wolves in Idaho. If biologists didn't detect a naturally occurring population of wolves after three years, the agencies would proceed with an experimental release there, too.

The state agencies and the livestock industry wouldn't hear of such a plan. They complained that our proposal didn't deal with northwestern Montana or provide enough certainty. How could they be sure that the agencies would keep their word? What if a legal challenge changed the rules? They also said that the proposal didn't shift enough management responsibility to the states.

The impasse over these two positions continued into April with no discernible progress. But at an April 10 meeting, the logjam finally showed signs of breaking. The committee decided that the only way to resolve the standoff was to vote on some proposals and set them aside if they didn't muster enough support.

Cool placed his proposal for removing wolves from the endangered species list on the floor first. The vote was five to four in favor, with one abstention. Congress had said the committee would have to cast six votes in favor of a proposal in order to ratify it. So, this proposal failed.

John Mumma, the Forest Service regional forester in the Northern Rockies, had refused to vote on the measure. Instead, he offered a compromise proposal that relied on the experimental population provision yet addressed many state agency and livestock industry concerns.

Mumma suggested extending the boundaries for the Yellowstone Park and Idaho experimental population areas to include all of Montana except for the northwestern part of the state in the immediate vicinity of Glacier Park. He proposed that state and federal agencies share wolf management responsibilities. To make sure the rules didn't change, he called for Congress to pass legislation ratifying the committee's final plan. He also proposed allowing landowners to shoot wolves they caught killing livestock.

The proposal was far from perfect. It was a compromise, but at least it seemed a starting point. It was late in the day. Committee members were tiring of the acrimonious debate, and the May 15 congressional deadline loomed. We approved Mumma's proposal nine to one. The livestock industry representative cast the only opposing vote, and we could see he'd wavered before doing so.

When the meeting broke up, the committee hadn't worked out some important details. Still, most of us left believing we'd at least built the framework of a final agreement. I felt good because at last the committee had begun to make some progress. We'd finish the plan at our final meeting, set for April 29 and 30 in Denver, Colorado.

For the next two weeks, representatives of various environmental groups bombarded me with opinions on the tentative deal. Some thought it a good compromise; others considered it too permissive.

I believed that the committee was heading in the right direction, but two points concerned me. My first objection was that the proposed experimental population boundaries extended too far into Montana. Congress intended for federal agencies to use the experimental population provision only where recovering an endangered species requires reintroduction and no populations of that species live. Mumma's proposed experimental population boundaries overlapped areas where wolves already were reproducing. I didn't think such boundaries could survive legal scrutiny.

My second major problem with the proposal was that it called for Congress to approve the document. In theory, I wasn't opposed to having Congress put its stamp of approval on the committee's work. But I knew from experience that anti-wolf politicians would use the approval requirement as an opportunity to meddle.

These were issues the committee could fix. But I had an even bigger problem. Defenders of Wildlife, my employer, was pressuring me to oppose the Mumma proposal because it would permit private landowners to kill wolves.

I was in a tight spot. On many occasions—on the livestock producers' trip to Minnesota, in speeches at conferences, and during several congressional meetings—I'd made it plain that the experimental population provision could allow private landowners to kill individual wolves that were attacking livestock, as long as killing the animals didn't inhibit the species' recovery. I'd researched the provision's legislative history and knew that Congress had made that point. Dave Mech and other scientists had reassured me that killing wolves under such conditions would have a negligible effect on the species' recovery. My support for private citizens' killing wolves was no secret within my organization. Defenders President Rupert Cutler backed this position.

Unbeknownst to me, less than a year earlier, Defenders' board of directors—without fully understanding the issue's complexities or its implications for Yellowstone Park wolf restoration—had adopted a resolution opposing any private killing of endangered species. Then, right before the Wolf Management Committee convened, Cutler left the organization. Now the organization's acting president—an eager-beaver lawyer named Jim Dougherty, who enjoyed a short career with Defenders—insisted that Defenders must oppose the Mumma proposal to let ranchers kill any wolves they saw attacking their livestock. The lawyers call this "private take."

I explained to Jim Dougherty (no relation to Tom Dougherty) that this was the ranchers' most important and emotional issue. I pointed out that allowing private take would have little effect on wolf recovery and that *any* plan the Wolf Management Committee approved was sure to include this provision. I also explained that I'd helped develop the provision specifically so we could avoid an even more permissive one. He still wouldn't hear of it.

The day before the meeting, he faxed me a curt message: "We have no choice but to vote against the plan. I know you disagree with this general position. I regret that I have to reemphasize that if your vote is contrary to the view of management, your employment status will be jeopardized. Sorry about this."

Jerry Jack hadn't seen his downfall coming. I saw mine.

I headed to the April 29 meeting in Denver uncertain what to do. Private take wasn't a big issue for the National Wildlife Federation and The Wolf Fund. I asked myself whether my status as a member of a government committee obliged me to represent the conservation community. Or was I free to represent the view of my own organization? I worried about eroding my credibility if I voted against an agreement I'd helped craft. My biggest question was whether I should do what was right—and risk my job—or take the safe course. On the airplane to Denver, my stomach churned. By then, I knew I'd probably take my chances and vote for the proposal.

My anxiety proved unnecessary. Other committee members

apparently had been under pressure, too. When the committee reconvened, our consensus had vanished. The state agencies and the livestock industry had regressed to their delist-the-wolf position. Mumma's proposal was dead.

The first day of the two-day meeting ended in deadlock; the next day was the last chance. The committee could send no recommendation to Congress if its members couldn't strike a deal.

Fish and Wildlife Service Director John Turner, back in his Washington, D.C., office, received word of the committee's stalemate. For several months, he'd been trying to knit an approach that state and federal agencies, the livestock industry, conservationists, and the Wyoming congressional delegation all could live with. He didn't want to see the Wolf Management Committee fail. He tried to do what the committee couldn't.

The next day, taking advantage of the time difference, he and some of his Washington staff got up early and devised a new compromise proposal. They faxed it to Denver, instructing the regional director to support it.

Turner's well-intentioned proposal was hurried and incomplete. He didn't have the advantage of the hours of committee discussion. He'd also bent too far backward trying to satisfy the hard-liners. Turner's desire for a recommendation to Congress—any recommendation—overcame his desire for a good one.

His plan had several major flaws. It would call on Congress to remove protection from wolves in northwestern Montana. It would use the experimental population provision in an area where wolves already existed. And it would let livestock producers shoot wolves on sight, regardless of whether the animals were preying on livestock.

I had no qualms about opposing the Turner plan, nor did Tom Dougherty. We warned other committee members that this proposal would get no support in Congress. Nevertheless, Cool and the representatives of the livestock industry and hunting interests went for the plan right away. After the Fish and Wildlife Service regional director switched his position, the representatives of the other agencies blindly followed suit—even the Park Service. Bill Mott would have been embarrassed. The other committee members outvoted us, eight to two.

Tom Dougherty and I had been right; the recommendation went nowhere. Legislation that turned the Endangered Species Act upside down had no chance of passage in the Democrat-controlled House and Senate. So, the Wolf Management Committee exercise proved yet another blind alley on the twisting path to Yellowstone Park wolf restoration.

After the committee fizzled, I headed to Washington, D.C., to visit Neal Sigmon, clerk of the House Interior Appropriations Subcommittee. By this time, he knew my line by heart: include funds in the appropriations bill to start an environmental impact statement on Yellowstone Park wolf restoration in 1992. We'd been through the drill before. Congressman Wayne Owens and Timm Kaminski hustled up support. Conservationists urged committee members to write letters to Subcommittee Chairman Sidney Yates. Once again, we succeeded; the bill cleared the House with $348,000 earmarked for an EIS.

Still, I lacked confidence. We'd been close so many times before. I felt like Tantalus, the Greek who'd tried to embarrass the gods and received their harshest punishment: placement for eternity in a pool of water in the hottest part of Hades. Whenever he bent down to soothe his parched throat, the water receded. Above the pool hung branches of trees laden with fruit. Whenever Tantalus tried to grasp a piece of fruit to relieve his hunger, the wind blew the branches out of reach.

But this time we weren't disappointed. No members from Montana, Idaho, or Wyoming sat on the Senate Appropriations Committee. McClure had retired. Although all six senators from the region had signed a letter against funding an EIS, no one on the committee would carry their water. Opponents had stalled this issue for four years, spending nearly one million dollars in the process. Now the committee had simply run out of reasons for saying no.

In November, Congress appropriated the funds. Work on the EIS would start in 1992. We'd finally dislodged the major impediment to wolf reintroduction.

THIRTEEN

WOLF WARS

In November 1991, the Fish and Wildlife Service surveyed its ranks for someone to lead the team that would prepare the environmental impact statement on restoring wolves to Yellowstone Park and central Idaho. The choice was obvious: Ed Bangs. Brick by brick, he'd built a Montana wolf recovery program so sturdy that even the biggest, baddest wolf opponents couldn't blow it down.

But Bangs was a reluctant hero. As much as he thrived on adversity, he wasn't sure he wanted the pressure-cooker EIS job. If he took it, he wanted to work independently, with no second-guessing from the regional and national offices of the Fish and Wildlife Service. Confident of Bangs's ability, his superiors agreed to his terms.

Bangs immediately assembled a team. He took on for himself the high-visibility roles of media spokesman, mollifier of irate politicians, and placater of angry citizens. Concepts, not details, are his strong suit. So, he found the consummate nuts-and-bolts person to be his right-hand man: Wayne Brewster, the former Fish and Wildlife Service endangered species leader who'd resuscitated the wolf recovery team. Brewster was now a Yellowstone Park biologist. Naturally meticulous, he kept lists, assigned tasks, and made sure nothing slipped through the cracks. His agency friends call him "the ultimate bureaucrat," and they mean it as a compliment.

Bangs chose Steve Fritts of the Fish and Wildlife Service as the team's resident science expert. Steady and precise, Fritts handled biological and technical matters—from defining a wolf population to planning how to reintroduce the species. He was the team's Dr. Science.

In addition, Bangs requisitioned Laird Robinson from the Forest Service to set up meetings and analyze public comment. Robinson isn't a typical bureaucrat. A former smokejumper, he has a contagious can-do style that inspires cooperation.

Other key members of the EIS team included representatives of Indian tribes, all three state wildlife agencies, and Animal Damage Control. Although the Fish and Wildlife Service took the lead, other federal agencies and all three states were closely involved.

Early in 1992, I called Bangs to discuss the upcoming EIS. Defenders of Wildlife and most other conservation groups were shifting gears, I said. For nearly a decade, we'd negotiated with wolf opponents to put together a workable plan. The Fish and Wildlife Service had a good idea what that plan was. Now we'd switched our emphasis to mobilizing wolf supporters to speak out for reintroduction.

Bangs had his line down pat. "This isn't going to be a voting contest," he said in his stiffest bureaucratic voice. This must have been the stock response he gave every wolf advocate or opponent who called. Indeed, the EIS process is supposed to be about information, not politics.

We both knew differently, though. Facts mattered, but political power mattered more. It *was* a voting contest, and if wolf advocates didn't outpoll the opposition, wolf reintroduction would never happen. I'd long ago lost my naiveté about saving wolves solely by enacting a law. As Abraham Lincoln once said, "Public sentiment is everything. With public sentiment, nothing can fail; without it, nothing can succeed."

Bangs's words about a "voting contest" stuck in my mind. Why not turn wolf reintroduction into an election? Why not put ballot boxes in Yellowstone Park? That's exactly what Defenders ended up doing as part of its "Vote Wolf!" campaign in the summers of 1992 and 1993.

First, I hired a person with organizational skills and a master's degree in wolf ecology to recruit and educate a host of volunteers. Next, Defenders' staff created a wolf display and brochure for use in the park. With the Park Service's permission, we set up our red, white, and blue booth in Yellowstone Park from June through September. Our volunteers urged visitors to vote for or against wolf restoration and place their ballots in a special box. They fielded visitors' questions and had the Fish and Wildlife Service send EIS information to any of them who wanted to become more involved in wolf recovery.

Meanwhile, Bangs and his team devised their own plan for talking with the public. Local members of Congress insisted that the agency provide many opportunities for local citizens to express their views. The politicians thought they could derail wolf reintroduction by giving opponents enough chances to shout down the plan.

The Fish and Wildlife Service didn't resist the politicians. In fact, it deluged the public with opportunities to comment. In April 1992, that agency, along with the Park Service and Forest Service, hosted thirty-four meetings—twenty-seven in Montana, Idaho, and Wyoming, the rest in seven cities across the country.

The meetings weren't conventional hearings but "open houses" at which citizens and biologists talked informally. It was an excellent way to educate people and seek their opinions on which issues the EIS should address.

The anti-wolf politicians were furious. This wasn't the raucous public participation they'd hoped for. They wanted conflict, not cooperation. In a letter to Secretary of the Interior Manuel Lujan, all seven Republican members of Congress from Montana, Idaho, and

Wyoming complained about the meetings. "Federal agencies clearly controlled the agenda," they protested. They demanded that the Fish and Wildlife Service hold formal public hearings—forums where angry people could shout into a microphone if they wished.

Montana Representative Ron Marlenee led the call for the kind of meetings where people could vent their anger. But he had more on his mind than wolves. After the 1990 census, reapportionment of congressional districts had cost Montana one of its two seats in the House of Representatives. That threw Marlenee into a winner-take-all race with his longtime foe Democratic Representative Pat Williams. Marlenee, convinced that most Montanans opposed Yellowstone Park wolf reintroduction, believed that stirring up controversy over wolves would boost his chances for reelection.

In an internal memo, Fish and Wildlife Service Director John Turner urged Secretary Lujan *not* to hold more public hearings. "We do not feel any additional meetings at this time will be in the public's or the taxpayer's best interest, as it is unlikely that they will result in any substantial difference in the identification of issues which need to be considered during this process," he wrote.

Turner also defended his agency's evenhanded approach to soliciting public comment. "This open house procedure reduces emotional conflict and controversy and is the best method for facilitating exchange of information between the agencies and the public," he maintained.

But Lujan, himself a former Republican congressman, folded like an umbrella. He announced that the Fish and Wildlife Service would conduct formal public hearings in August 1992 in Cheyenne, Wyoming; Helena, Montana; Boise, Idaho; Salt Lake City, Utah; Seattle, Washington; and Washington, D.C. Conservationists and wolf opponents would face off in those cities. As in Civil War battles, opponents would form skirmish lines, fire, and then see who had the most people left standing.

Thus far, the National Wildlife Federation, Defenders, and The Wolf Fund had done most of the work on wolf conservation. But the planned hearings galvanized environmental groups across the region, including the Sierra Club, the National Audubon Society, The Wilderness Society, The Wolf Education and Research Center, the Idaho Conservation League, and the Greater Yellowstone Coalition. The war over wolves was taking another dramatic turn.

After several conference calls, the conservation generals decided how to mass and deploy the troops. All groups would send alerts and make phone calls to their foot soldiers. Larger groups would rent buses to transport troops. The wolf army would mass at rallies before every hearing at each state capital or major city. Then we'd charge.

Like wars of old, this one featured plenty of fanfare. At the Helena rally, the entertainment included music, orators, even a live wolf. Before a crowd of several hundred people, I introduced movie star Andie MacDowell, whose western Montana ranch is home to wild wolves. Next, Montana writer Rick Bass read a short passage from his book *The Ninemile Wolves*, and Tom France of the National Wildlife Federation revved up the crowd.

Down the street, the anti-wolf crowd held a competing rally, then marched to the civic center brandishing signs. One asked, "How Would You Like to Have Your Ass Eaten Off by a Wolf?" Another proclaimed, "The Wolf Is the Saddam Hussein of the Animal World." Nothing subtle here.

Nearly eight hundred people squeezed into the civic center for the hearing. Armed guards manned the doors. Bright yellow and black signs at the entrances announced, "OFFICIAL FEDERAL HEARING—No Alcohol—No Signs—No Weapons—No Animals." Inside, people wearing Patagonia jackets jostled others wearing cowboy hats. Everyone was edgy. Officials told the audience not to boo or cheer, for what little good that did.

Elected officeholders spoke first. To everyone's surprise, Congressman Marlenee didn't show up. Instead, he sent an aide with a prepared statement that was vintage Marlenee: a diatribe against wolves, wilderness, and welfare ending with a call for Fish and Wildlife Service Director Turner's head on a platter. Some audience members cheered. Others booed. Federal officials exchanged nervous looks.

The tenor of the hearing changed when Jack Gladstone, a Native American singer who supports wolf restoration, made a statement on behalf of the Blackfeet Nation. Accompanying himself on the guitar, he sang "Circle of Life," his song about the connection among wolves, humans, and other animals. His eloquence settled the crowd.

It was quite a day for speechmaking. Over the next eight hours, about one hundred people spoke out about wolves. "Wolves do not kill people," one person asserted. "Fatty beef does." Someone from the other camp didn't mince words, declaring that "Only a brain-dead son of a bitch would favor reintroduction of wolves." By the end of the day, about 60 percent of the speakers had come out in favor of wolves, 40 percent against.

Ironically, these politically motivated hearings instigated by wolf opponents led to a stunning victory for wolf advocates. It was hard to believe, but support for wolves in Cheyenne ran nearly as high as in Seattle and the nation's capital. Overall, nearly 80 percent of the people who spoke at the hearings backed wolf restoration.

The hearings turned the tide in favor of wolf restoration, demonstrating the depth and breadth of wolf support around the country and even in Montana, Idaho, and Wyoming. In November 1992, Congressman Marlenee, having misread the attitudes of Montanans—including their sentiments about wolves—lost his seat to Congressman Williams. The support for wolves shown by these initial hearings also caused most livestock industry groups to throw in the towel. A marked attendance decline at later hearings testified to their flagging interest in battling wolves.

Just before the hearings, an even more unexpected event had occurred. In August, a visitor filmed a large black canid—looking for all the world like a wolf—feeding on a bison carcass in Yellowstone Park. Then, in September, a hunter killed a black animal with different markings from the filmed wolf about two miles south of the park; genetic tests later confirmed it to be a wolf.

These sightings were a bombshell that prompted some conservationists to question the necessity of reintroduction. Wolves transplanted to the park probably would be designated by the government as an experimental population. That designation would create more flexible rules for managing the wolves. The problem was that many conservationists considered "flexible" synonymous with "weaker." Wolves naturally recolonizing the park couldn't be considered experimental. They'd enjoy the full legal protection of the Endangered Species Act.

The movie footage made national news, creating an uproar that lasted several months. It didn't matter that there still was no evidence of an established population of wolves in the park, despite more than one hundred sightings there over the past twenty years. People wanted to believe that wolves had returned.

The possibility that wolves had made it to Yellowstone Park on their own muddied the waters for reintroduction. Few people remembered how similar uncertainty over the presence of wolves in the park in the early 1970s had kept the Park Service from moving forward with reintroduction then. Even conservationists seemed to forget that a debate over the question of whether there were wolves in central Idaho had been running for more than a decade. Occasional sightings of individual wolves bolstered some people's hopes for natural recovery, but it simply wasn't happening. A man speaking for the livestock industry inadvertently summed up my frustration with natural recovery: "The industry supports natural recovery," he said. "It's been working for the past ten years." From a stockman's perspective, it had worked. For Yellowstone Park, "natural wolf recovery" might mean no recovery.

The idea that wolves might be living in the park largely undetected didn't wash. After all, identifying the first pioneering wolves in Montana—the Magic Pack—had been fairly easy. The animals weren't particularly secretive. Many Montanans saw packs of wolves, heard them howling, found their kills, or discovered their tracks. Especially in winter, wolves and their sign were quite visible. In 1992, using the same techniques for evaluating sightings that biologists had used in Idaho and Yellowstone Park, the Fish and Wildlife Service had discovered at least five packs of wolves in Montana. The odds of a wolf pack's living undetected in the park were nil.

There was a simple solution to the confusion over the possible presence of wolves. The question wasn't whether a lone wolf or two had made it to the park. It was whether Yellowstone Park once again had a resident wolf *population.* All the Fish and Wildlife Service needed to do was define what constituted a wolf population. Then the government could decide to reintroduce wolves on the basis of whether such a population was present.

Team scientist Steve Fritts went about the job of defining what, exactly, comprises a wolf population. He consulted two dozen of North America's leading wolf experts, who concluded that reproduction was the key factor in determining the presence of wolves. Fritts, incorporating their suggestions, defined the minimum standards for a wolf population as at least two breeding pairs of animals that survived and produced pups for two years. This definition finally placed sightings of individual wolves in perspective: although interesting, they weren't very important in the grand scheme of restoring wolves unless biologists detected breeding.

In July 1993, the Fish and Wildlife Service and fellow agencies drafted an EIS. It analyzed several alternatives, ranging from *not* reintroducing wolves to Yellowstone Park to reintroducing them under the strictest terms possible under the Endangered Species Act. Its "preferred alternative" called for reintroducing wolves as an experimental population. This alternative involved no land-use restrictions; it would let private landowners kill wolves in the act of attacking their livestock; and federal and state agencies would share management of the wolves. The document held no big surprises.

The agency's preferred alternative proved that the Wolf Management Committee's exercise hadn't been pointless. The alternative was middle ground that the committee had identified but couldn't bring itself to endorse.

From the committee's deliberations, the Fish and Wildlife Service had learned which wolf management concerns were deal-breakers. The preferred alternative would avoid them. It would allow ranchers to kill wolves but only in the narrowest of circumstances; it would establish large experimental population areas but keep them separate from Montana's existing wolf population; and it would require approval by the secretary of the interior but not Congress.

The only surprise was the Fish and Wildlife Service's application of the plan to central Idaho as well as Yellowstone Park. The agency took this stance because of lack of firm evidence of wolf reproduction in central Idaho. In fact, even though Idaho is nearer existing wolf populations, the number of sightings recorded there was similar to that in the Yellowstone area. The recommendation was an interesting development and perhaps Senator McClure's most enduring legacy. Government agencies pushed central Idaho reintroduction even more aggressively than did conservation groups.

Defenders, The Wolf Fund, and the National Wildlife Federation hailed the preferred alternative as a major step forward. Several conservation groups, however, attacked use of the experimental population provision, saying it didn't give wolves enough protection. Doug Honnold, a lawyer with the Sierra Club Legal Defense Fund, called the preferred alternative illegal and threatened to sue the Fish and Wildlife Service. He told a Jackson, Wyoming, newspaper that individual wolves could be considered an existing population. "I think you can have a population of one," he said.

Honnold and a few other environmentalists believed that experimental reintroduction would be bad for wolves. Some conservationists advocated the most protective alternative—reintroducing wolves classified as "fully endangered," not as an experimental population—purely for strategic reasons. Taking this extreme position made the experimental population alternative the middle ground. It was a standard negotiating tactic: to get what you need, ask for more than you really want.

The disagreement among environmentalists didn't overly

concern the Fish and Wildlife Service. The agency's preferred alternative had garnered considerable support across the region. In 1993 and 1994, editorials calling the agency's proposal a reasonable compromise appeared in most major newspapers in Montana, Idaho, and Wyoming. A *Bozeman Chronicle* editorial summed up the general thinking: "A hard pill to swallow, but the best medicine for stockmen just the same."

State governments also seemed content with the preferred alternative because it made them full partners in wolf management. Making state wildlife agency biologists part of the EIS team paid a dividend: no state government actively opposed the suggested reintroductions.

Even the Republican politicians had mellowed. In July 1993, Wyoming Senators Malcolm Wallop and Alan Simpson indicated in the Casper *Star-Tribune* that they grudgingly accepted the reintroduction proposal. "If we're going to have it shoved down our throats," Simpson said, "it should be done as an experimental population so we have the proper management flexibility."

Livestock organizations could read the tea leaves. They didn't like or support wolf restoration, but they no longer thought they could win the war against their age-old enemy. The major industry groups dropped their over-my-dead-body stand. The exceptions were the Wyoming Farm Bureau Federation and its Montana, Idaho, and national counterparts. They, along with Troy Mader of the Abundant Wildlife Society and Arlene Hanson of the Cody, Wyoming-based No-Wolf Option Committee, continued to organize opponents to speak out against wolf restoration. These groups were rowing hard, but their ship was sinking.

Wolf advocates outnumbered opponents at nearly every public hearing held on the draft EIS. Despite differences of opinion concerning the document, conservation groups continued to work together to turn out people for the hearings, sending mailings to their members asking them to submit comments on the EIS.

When the official public comment period on the draft EIS closed in the fall of 1993, the Fish and Wildlife Service had received over 160,000 comments. According to Bangs, the EIS raked in more public comment than any similar document ever prepared in the United States.

Defenders' "Vote Wolf!" project in Yellowstone Park yielded more than seventy thousand of those comments. In October 1993, we delivered to the Interior Department ballots from park visitors from all fifty states and more than twenty-five foreign countries. All but about two thousand had voted in favor of reintroduction. Wolves had also won a landslide victory at the ballot box.

It had taken years for people working inside and outside government to get the EIS launched. Once they managed to do so, the process worked. The Fish and Wildlife Service and the other agencies laid out the facts, analyzed the likely effects on people and their environment, and listened to what the public had to say about it all. The result was a decision to do the right thing. In June 1994, the Fish and Wildlife Service released the final EIS, and Interior Secretary Bruce Babbitt approved it. The agency planned to capture wolves in Alberta, Canada, in November and release them in Yellowstone Park and central Idaho.

The fall of 1994 should have been the time when conservationists pushed together to ensure that wolf reintroduction would become a reality. Defenders, The Wolf Fund, and the National Wildlife Federation saw the reintroduction plan as a practical way to return wolves to Yellowstone Park and Idaho. This was our chance to prove that the Endangered Species Act could resolve even the thorniest issues. Doing so could help defuse mounting criticism in Congress regarding the act.

But the Sierra Club Legal Defense Fund, Sierra Club, and National Audubon Society saw things differently. They couldn't abide an experimental population designation for wolves in Idaho. In early September, they announced plans to sue the Fish and Wildlife Service over the central Idaho reintroduction. I'd always expected that someone would file a lawsuit over wolf restoration, but I never thought my friends would do it.

"It's not a wolf-saving plan, it's a wolf-killing plan," Honnold, the Sierra Club Legal Defense Fund lawyer, claimed in a news release accompanying the organization's notice of intent to sue. "The FWS plan ignores the biology of wolves and what we need to do to accomplish true recovery," he told a *High Country News* reporter. "As soon as a wolf crosses Interstate 90 (the boundary of the experimental population area), it becomes open season."

I was inured to Troy Mader's and the Farm Bureau's blatant disregard for truth. As Winston Churchill observed of an opponent, "Occasionally he stumbled over the truth, but hastily picked himself up as if nothing had happened." But my fellow conservationists' indifference to facts raised my hackles.

The Legal Defense Fund's assertions didn't hold up under scrutiny. Its claim that the preferred alternative didn't represent sound science was contradicted by a letter to the Fish and Wildlife Service. Sixteen of North America's leading wolf scientists described that alternative as a "practical plan that meets the needs of state governments and local residents while facilitating prompt, effective and economical wolf recovery."

The scientists viewed the experimental population provision as an asset, not a liability. "We believe the additional management flexibility afforded through the experimental population provision will enhance public acceptance of wolf recovery, which in turn should result in reduced illegal killing," they said in a letter to the Fish and Wildlife Service.

The plan certainly wouldn't permit an open season on wolves, as the Legal Defense Fund's lawyer had implied. Ranchers could shoot wolves only on private property and only if they caught the animals killing livestock. Furthermore, if a rancher killed a wolf, he'd be required to report it within twenty-four hours and present evidence of dead or injured livestock. Failing to follow the rules would invite federal prosecution.

Experimental reintroduction would restore wolves more quickly, with much greater assurance, and at less cost than would a highly uncertain natural recovery. It would focus reintroduction on national parks and wilderness areas, where conflicts would be minimal. I recalled Senator McClure's concern that some environmentalists might use wolves as a smoke screen for other items on their agendas, such as logging restrictions and wilderness preservation. There was more than a germ of truth to what McClure had said.

I was all for protecting wildlife habitat; I'd been involved in that fight for seventeen years. But Mech and other scientists had made it clear that additional habitat protection wasn't necessary to restoring wolves to Yellowstone Park and Idaho. Montana's experience with wolf recovery supported that conclusion. Land managers had imposed no land-use restrictions because of wolves, yet wolf populations increased at about 20 percent a year in the state.

The actual differences between managing wolves as an *endangered* population and as an *experimental* one were minuscule. Such details held meaning for lawyers, not wolves.

But even legal experts didn't agree with the Legal Defense Fund. "Their legal theory is simply wrong," Tom France said. "Congress wrote the experimental population provision to promote flexible programs for endangered species recovery, and that's exactly what's been accomplished with the wolf reintroduction effort."

Renée Askins of The Wolf Fund said it best: "Laws don't protect wolves; people protect wolves. Greater protection of wolves is not necessarily achieved through more restrictive laws." The goodwill generated by addressing the concerns of local people would save far more wolves than any number of carefully worded laws.

The Legal Defense Fund didn't seek an injunction to halt the reintroductions. Its goal wasn't to stop reintroduction but to have a judge declare that the reintroduced wolves were endangered animals, not experimental ones. It refused to acknowledge that such legal sleight of hand would enrage locals and might cause them to vent their frustration on the wolves.

Environmental factions weren't the only ones objecting to the wolf restoration plan. In late September, the Wyoming Farm Bureau announced that it, too, planned to sue the Fish and Wildlife Service. Its arguments sounded remarkably similar to those of the Legal Defense Fund. Besides protesting the experimental population designation, the Farm Bureau contended that the Fish and Wildlife Service planned to introduce the wrong wolf subspecies—not that the group would have dreamed of supporting the right one. The organization based its argument on the obsolete wolf classifications devised in 1944 by Stanley Young and Edward Goldman. The tactic was a sign that wolf opponents were running out of ammunition.

Bangs and his EIS team were on overload throughout September and October, responding to legal threats, preparing final rules for managing the experimental population, and organizing a team to capture wolves in Canada. For weeks on end, EIS team members worked twelve-hour days seven days a week, rushing to transplant wolves to Yellowstone Park and Idaho by the end of 1994.

I caught Bangs on the telephone late on one of these days. He was obviously tired and stressed-out. Wolves were no longer fun. "My life is a black pit of despair," he said. This from the most cheerful person I knew, a man who thrives on pressure and controversy.

But Bangs and company—especially Wayne Brewster—managed to get their work done. By November, they'd finished the rules and prepared all the necessary documents in response to the legal threats. Biologists, working with Canadian trappers, had captured, fitted with radio collars, and released back to the wild seventeen wolves from thirteen packs in Canada. The radio collars would make it easier to find the packs later, when it was time to transplant them to Yellowstone Park and Idaho. Operation Wolfstock was set to go.

Meanwhile, the Wyoming Farm Bureau continued seeking a way to block reintroduction. Aided by lawyers from the Mountain States Legal Foundation—a law firm founded by James Watt—the Farm Bureau filed a lawsuit in late November. The Fish and Wildlife Service voluntarily agreed to postpone bringing wolves to Yellowstone Park or Idaho until a judge could respond to the Farm Bureau's request for a preliminary injunction. The showdown took place a few days before Christmas in U.S. District Court in Cheyenne.

"In the old days, things were much simpler," Ed Bangs told me. "If someone disagreed with you, he'd find the nearest tree and string you up. Now people are much crueler; they take you to court."

To win an injunction halting wolf reintroduction, the Farm Bureau had to convince Judge William Downes that its members would suffer "irreparable harm" if wolves were released. Its best shot at doing so was to show that wolves would cause ranchers significant economic hardship.

The government defense rested on a three-legged stool: wolves kill livestock infrequently; government agents would kill or remove ones that kill livestock; and Defenders, using money from its Wolf Compensation Fund, would pay livestock producers market value for all verified losses.

The government presented four witnesses. Bangs and Mech presented the livestock-loss information and discussed government programs for managing wolves. Carter Niemeyer of Animal Damage Control told how government biologists would stop wolf predation if it occurred. And I explained Defenders' Wolf Compensation Fund.

The Farm Bureau presented five witnesses—all ranchers. Although they were sincere, forthright people who elicited sympathy from the judge, they presented only fears, not facts. I wondered whether they realized that the Farm Bureau had paid more money in legal fees in this lawsuit than Defenders had spent compensating Montana ranchers over the past seven years.

It wasn't even a close call. On January 3, 1995, Judge Downes denied the Farm Bureau's request for an injunction. After years of struggle and maneuvering, we'd finally cleared the last obstacle to reintroduction. Now it was time to return wolves to their ancestral homeland.

FOURTEEN

BACK TO THE WILD

O̶n Thursday, January 12, 1995, I was barreling down Montana's Interstate 90 at a steady eighty-five miles an hour. Racing the sunrise, I was intent on witnessing a milestone in wildlife conservation history: the return of wolves to Yellowstone Park.

I was running late. Until a few hours earlier, I'd planned to attend the release of wolves into Idaho's Frank Church-River of No Return Wilderness. With wolves originally destined for Yellowstone Park and central Idaho that same day, practicality had pushed me toward Idaho. Defenders of Wildlife President Rodger Schlickeisen and Media Director Joan Moody were already in Yellowstone Park, so my presence there wasn't essential. I'd also thought that the wolves' release in Idaho would be more dramatic. Idaho reintroduction plans called for a "hard" release; the cage doors would open, and the wolves— unrelated young adults of breeding age—would dash to freedom. In the park, family groups of wolves would be delivered to one-acre pens, where they'd spend at least eight weeks getting used to their new surroundings before wildlife managers would free them.

But on Wednesday night, the weather took a turn for the worse in my hometown of Missoula, Montana—the stopover point for flying the Canadian wolves to Idaho aboard a Forest Service transport plane. Dense fog promised to ground the plane, delaying the release of wolves into the Idaho wilderness. Prospects for a Thursday release receded with the visibility.

I automatically began calculating hours and distances. I wanted to be there when the first wolves arrived in Yellowstone Park.

Most environmental issues don't have distinct beginnings or endings. Too often, it's unclear whether a battle has been won, lost, or postponed. This time, things were different. I wanted to see those wolves hit the finish line. I'd suffered through too many bad moments during the past fifteen years not to be there for the best one.

I made a few quick phone calls. The Park Service was trucking wolves from Great Falls, Montana, to the park Wednesday night. W-Day for Yellowstone Park would stay on schedule: 8 A.M. Thursday, fog or no fog. I had time to make the three hundred-mile drive, even on roads so slick the National Weather Service advised emergency travel only. Late Wednesday night, I jumped into my car and pointed it east.

And so it happened that, early the next morning, I was speeding up Paradise Valley toward the park's northern entrance, frantically checking my watch. I was less than ten miles away, but it was almost 8 A.M. My heart sank as I rounded a corner and saw a police car puttering down the road in front of me. This had to be the world's worst timing. Speeding fines on Montana highways run you just five dollars, but tickets take time to write. As I stood on my brakes to avoid rear-ending the patrol car, I knew that a ticket would cost me more than five dollars; it would also cost me my chance to watch a historic event unfold.

Then I saw the car up close. It wasn't the Montana Highway Patrol, after all, but a Park Service ranger. Rangers don't enforce speed limits outside national parks, so I roared by with a sigh of relief. The ranger squinted hard at me as I zoomed past.

Blasting around the next curve along the sinuous Yellowstone

River, I ran into more bad luck: a slow-moving horse trailer blocking the highway. I'd never get by.

Bad luck? It took just a moment to realize I'd landed smack in the middle of the wolf train, the procession of government vehicles bringing the wolves to the park. I drove behind the trailer for about a mile. When the driver eased off the road into a pullout, I followed suit. Suddenly, two Park Service patrol cars appeared out of nowhere and cut me off, front and back. Two uniformed rangers approached me, their hands tensed beside their firearms. Suspicion was written all over their faces. Clearly, they took me for trouble—maybe a zealous member of the Wyoming Farm Bureau staging a last-ditch stunt to stop the reintroduction.

"I'm on their side," I said quickly, motioning toward the crates of wolves inside the horse trailer. One of the rangers recognized me at last, and everyone relaxed. Only later did I learn I'd thrown a big scare into a special Park Service SWAT team responsible for protecting the wolves. The rangers smiled and said they'd be taking the wolves into the park within half an hour. Off I went.

I parked my car in Gardiner, within sight of one of Yellowstone Park's most recognizable manmade features—the towering stone monument known as the Roosevelt Arch. President Theodore Roosevelt dedicated this entrance to the park in 1903. As I walked through, I stopped to read its inscription: "For the benefit and enjoyment of the people—Yellowstone National Park, created by an act of Congress, March 1, 1872." It's curious how time has so changed our perception of wolves and their public benefit.

It's impossible to stand in the shadow of the Roosevelt Arch and not be filled with a sense of history. Many presidents and other famous people have passed through this portal. Meeting the wolves there had a touch of irony. For all Theodore Roosevelt's great passion for wildlife and the outdoors, he was no fan of wolves. In his book *Wilderness Hunter*, he described the wolf as "the beast of waste and desolation."

But restoring wolves to Yellowstone Park has been defined by historical ironies. The very agencies that eliminated the wolf from the park nearly seventy years earlier—the National Park Service and the precursor of the Fish and Wildlife Service—now were the strongest advocates of reintroduction. Coincidentally, it took government agencies just about as long to restore wolves as it had taken to eliminate them—about twenty years.

Hundreds of people standing near the arch began shouting as the horse trailer and Park Service patrol cars appeared on the horizon. My longtime partner in wolf recovery efforts, Renée Askins, jumped up and down yelling, "Here they come! Here they come!" I hugged her and said, "I told you it wasn't going to be *that* hard." We both laughed.

The crowd cheered as the government vehicles snaked through Gardiner. Television cameras were everywhere, and Park Service employees and Gardiner schoolchildren had joined the festivities. I watched an *NBC Nightly News* team interview some kids.

"What do you think about all this?" the reporter boomed, thrusting a microphone into the freckled face of a twelve-year-old boy. "Why, I think it's hist—orical," he said, almost blurting out "hysterical."

As the trucks neared the arch, I worried about what might go wrong. A flat tire? A wolf-seeking missile launched by our adversaries? After a decade of fighting for wolf recovery, I'd come to expect the worst.

But nothing went wrong—not yet, anyhow. As the trucks passed through the arch, those of us near the gate let out a big howl to greet the park's newest residents. No one minded that the wolves didn't respond. The procession slowed to let Secretary of the Interior Bruce Babbitt and Fish and Wildlife Service Director Mollie Beattie get out and greet the crowd.

Television camera crews immediately descended on them. "This is a day of redemption and a day of hope," Babbitt proclaimed. "It's a day when the limits of what is possible have been greatly expanded because we are showing our children that restoration is possible, that we can restore a community to its natural state." He and other federal officials then began the forty-mile trek to deliver the eight wolves to the acclimation pens in the Lamar Valley, between Mammoth and Cooke City.

But just when it seemed the wolves had hit the finish line, a federal judge extended the marathon. The Wyoming Farm Bureau—still smarting from losing its legal skirmish in Cheyenne—wasn't done fighting. At the last possible moment the day before, the organization had filed an emergency appeal in the Tenth Circuit Court of Appeals, in Denver. The court granted a forty-eight-hour stay barring release of wolves into Yellowstone Park and central Idaho. Although such stays are routine, giving judges time to review a case, the potential effect of this delay was anything but routine. As Interior Department lawyers saw it, the stay even prohibited releasing the wolves from their cramped travel crates into the one-acre, highly secure acclimation pens.

The Farm Bureau and its allies could have filed their appeal anytime in the two previous weeks. Instead, they waited until the wolves were actually on their way to the park and central Idaho. This last-minute legal chicanery smacked of obstructionism and was widely viewed by the media and public as downright mean-spirited.

More to the point, the legal maneuver created additional and unnecessary hardship for the animals. The order required the Park Service to keep the wolves in their two-by-four-by-three-foot metal crates while the court reviewed the case. The wolves' capture, their intensive handling by humans, and their long journey from Canada had been extremely stressful for them. Agency veterinarians voiced concern about how the animals would fare if confined much longer.

Federal officials could do nothing more than put the eight wolves inside the enclosures, still in their crates, and wait as Justice Department lawyers in Denver fought to lift the stay.

There the wolves sat for most of Thursday. Persecuted in this country for more than a century, they now suffered their final indignity amid what otherwise was a national celebration.

Babbitt was somber at an afternoon news conference. "If we

don't get those wolves out of those cages, they may turn into coffins," he said. Defenders President Rodger Schlickeisen told the hundred or more reporters, "While the Farm Bureau may not want wolves in Yellowstone Park, the American public does. Let's free the Yellowstone Eight!"

The wolves finally tasted freedom that night under the shimmer of an almost full moon. After the court lifted the stay around 7 P.M., Wayne Brewster and other Park Service biologists set about releasing the wolves. By now, the animals had languished in their cages for over thirty-six hours. At about 10:30 P.M., the cages were opened. Soon afterward, wolf paws hit the powdery Yellowstone Park snow.

That same night, I once again was zooming down Interstate 90, this time heading back to Missoula. The Idaho reintroduction was on for Friday, and there was room for me on the plane headed for the wilderness landing strip where the Fish and Wildlife Service planned to release the wolves. I pulled into Missoula in the middle of the night, caught a few hours sleep, and was at the airport by 7 A.M.

Like many best-laid schemes of wolves and men, this one went awry. The fog that had gripped Missoula when I left still hadn't cleared. At dawn, it was obvious that no planes would fly. Laird Robinson, the Forest Service public affairs person handling logistics, said the wolves would be trucked to Salmon, Idaho, and flown from there to the wilderness release site.

So, off I drove down the icy road toward Salmon, four hours south of Missoula. Accompanying me were two of my favorite veterans of the wolf wars, fellow conservationists Tom France, still with the National Wildlife Federation, and Pat Tucker. Tucker had left that organization a couple of years earlier to start Wild Sentry, a nonprofit group dedicated to educating the public about wolves. Over the years, France had become one of the region's most respected conservation lawyers.

We passed the time by trading war stories.

"Remember the first time we discussed wolves with Conrad Burns in D.C.?" Tucker asked.

Of course I did. We weren't two minutes into our meeting when the Republican senator from Montana pulled his portly frame out of his chair, hitched up his pants, and wagged his finger in our faces. "I'll tell you one thing for sure," he said. "If they reintroduce wolves to Yellowstone Park, there will be a dead child within a year."

"I guess the clock starts running today," Tucker observed. "Who's going to write him a letter next year reminding him his prediction didn't come true?"

"Now I've got a question for you," I said. "Wolf restoration's been a long time coming. What do you think were the main turning points along the way?"

"Getting the recovery plan signed in 1987," France said without hesitation. "That was huge. It took us more than five years."

I reminded them how the wolves had begun killing livestock near Browning soon afterward. "If they'd laid into those cows and sheep just a few weeks earlier," I said, "we'd still be trying to get it signed."

"But reintroduction didn't really take off until agencies proved they'd control depredation," France pointed out. "Defenders' compensation fund has made a difference, too. It saved our bacon in Cheyenne with the Farm Bureau lawsuit."

"Hey, money talks," I said. "It was definitely a big factor in getting the EIS started. Maybe getting Congress to appropriate money for that was the real key to restoration. Without specific congressional direction, agencies could have kept on doing what they'd done for twenty years: give in to the Alan Simpsons and Malcolm Wallops of the world."

We still hadn't talked about the major players in restoring wolves to Yellowstone Park. "Who do you think are the real heroes?" I asked.

Tucker nominated Ed Bangs. "He never let the EIS wander off track," she said. "He did an incredible job of keeping everyone motivated. Whenever there was a problem, he'd fix it."

"Sure, Ed's done great work," France said, "but he's a newcomer compared with people like Wayne Brewster and John Varley."

"Don't forget John Weaver," I said. "He carried the freight on the recovery team when no one else would."

But my top choice unquestionably was William Penn Mott, the inspiring former Park Service director. "He made Yellowstone wolves his cause back when there was no political support, just because it was the right thing to do," I said. "He took a big risk that probably cost him his job." I told Tucker and France what became of Mott. Instead of quitting the Park Service when President Bush didn't reappoint him, he took a fairly low-level public relations job with the agency. Before he died in 1992, he helped secure Park Service protection for one of the last wild places along San Francisco Bay. He was pure of heart to the end.

France thought Renée Askins deserves major recognition, too. "She's been absolutely phenomenal at getting national media attention for Yellowstone wolves." When conservationists were pushing for the EIS, articles on Yellowstone Park wolf restoration appeared in dozens of national publications, including *Newsweek, Time, People*, and *Life*. Askins was the one who'd inspired people to write most of those stories. The media have always loved her literary style, her romantic flair.

"Yes," Tucker agreed, "and she never let up the pressure on agencies."

I suggested a person I knew would be controversial. "How about Jim McClure?" I asked.

"That's interesting," France said thoughtfully. "But I'm not sure. We'd probably still be trying to get an EIS started if he hadn't finally retired."

"Could be," I replied. "But McClure was the one who legitimized wolf recovery not just for Yellowstone but for Idaho, too. When every other politician ran for cover—even our Democratic friends—he stood up for wolves, helping us keep the reintroduction issue alive."

"Maybe," Tucker said. "But I'm still not really sure what he was up to. Let's call him a dark hero."

Before we knew it, we were on the outskirts of Salmon. Dozens of reporters and wolf fans waited at the airport when we arrived. But once again, the gods didn't smile on wolves or their supporters. Low clouds settled over the mountains encircling the Salmon River. The animals would have to wait another day, and so would we.

The next afternoon—January 14, 1995—the Fish and Wildlife Service released four wolves on the edge of the Frank Church-River of No Return Wilderness. Within a week, the agency released eleven more wolves transplanted from Canada into the Idaho wilderness area and six more into acclimation pens at Yellowstone Park.

A few weeks later, at the Park Service's invitation, I was sitting on an elk carcass in the back of an old wooden sled drawn by two mules, heading in to see the wolves at the Crystal Bench acclimation pen. The Park Service biologists planned to feed the road-killed elk to the wolves, and I could walk to a ridge top a few hundred yards away and watch. The wolves were in an enclosure at the bottom of the hill.

It was a cold February morning, and I welcomed the chance to warm my body by climbing the steep ridge. I tramped up the slope, crossing dozens of elk and bison tracks. As I crested the hill, I caught a glimpse of six wolves led by a large, silver-throated black animal holding his tail high in the air. They made a stirring black-and-white portrait as they dashed through a thick stand of ivory-colored aspens. My first impression matched a vision of wildness I'd carried in my head a long time.

These aren't paper wolves, I thought; wolf reintroduction is actually happening. The years of recovery plans, environmental impact statements, and trips to Washington, D.C., had taken on a flesh and blood form.

I stayed on the ridge just a few minutes. The wolves didn't feed while I watched but constantly ran around in the enclosure. They repeatedly tested the fence, searching for an opening. The Park Service was giving the wolves first-class treatment, but it was easy to see that escape was on their mind.

Traveling down the Lamar Valley on the way back to park headquarters in Mammoth, I slowed the car several times to let bison cross the road. Hordes of elk covered every windswept hillside. These elk and bison had a surprise in store for them. For the Canadian wolves, being transplanted to Yellowstone Park was like winning the lupine lottery. Surely, nowhere else in North America would they have an easier time finding food. It will be fascinating to watch the new relationships unfold.

I pulled over at a small turnout overlooking where Hellroaring Creek joins the Yellowstone River. It was here that Vernon Bailey of the Biological Survey discovered one of the park's last wolf dens in March 1916. The wolves had dug several burrows into the open hillside on the west side of the creek. The den apparently had been used for many years; Bailey reported finding dozens of old elk skulls scattered nearby.

Bailey and his men tried to shoot the adult wolves but missed. The wolves moved their pups about a mile upslope, to a natural cave among loose rocks. The persistent government agents weren't to be denied; they finally killed three adults and six pups.

I sat on the hillside on the far side of the valley trying to piece the episode together. Eight decades later, the scene had changed very little. The same grassy slope led to the same rocky cliffs. I wondered whether Yellowstone Park's new wolves might rediscover this bygone denning spot.

Yellowstone Park really is a perfect home for wolves, I thought as I gazed upon the land sprawling for miles below me. Hundreds of elk wandered near the river, their tracks crisscrossing the landscape. Small herds of bison dotted the hillsides. They plowed the snow off the hard ground with their broad heads, seeking stems of nourishment. Through my binoculars, I could see clouds of vapor rising from their nostrils. Only one species of the park's original fauna was missing—but not for long.

On March 21, 1995, Park Service biologists began releasing the wolves from their pens. The metal gates swung open, and Yellowstone Park was on the road to being whole once more.

E P I L O G U E

No one declared a truce in the wolf wars, even after wolves had returned to Yellowstone Park and central Idaho. In fact, the battle cries grew shriller than ever. The Wyoming legislature, dominated by agricultural interests, welcomed wolves with a $500 bounty for anyone who managed to shoot one straying outside park boundaries. The governor vetoed the bounty but not the sentiment behind it. Montana's legislature responded with a resolution calling for the government to stock New York's Central Park with wolves. Idaho's new governor threatened to call out the National Guard to drive the wolves from his state.

More serious and worrisome was the new crop of representatives and senators arriving in Washington, D.C., around the time the wolves arrived in Yellowstone Park and Idaho. The November 1994 elections ended forty years of Democratic domination of Congress. Swept out of power was the party that had created and defended the Endangered Species Act and grudgingly made possible the restoration of wolves in the Northern Rockies. Swept into power was a Republican majority whose members included many outspoken critics of endangered species protection. The herculean efforts that Ed Bangs, Wayne Brewster, and other people had made in the fall of 1994 had proved crucial. They'd made it possible to reintroduce the wolves to Yellowstone Park and Idaho before the political winds blew shut the window of opportunity.

As soon as they took office in January, new representatives from Wyoming and Idaho demanded a congressional hearing on the wolf reintroductions. The new kids on the block flexed their muscles. Wolf-bashing became fashionable once again.

This renewed congressional opposition forewarned conservationists of a battle over shipping more wolves to Yellowstone Park and Idaho. The reintroduction plan called for releasing in each area fifteen wolves a year for as many as five years running or until a wild wolf population was established. It would take a miracle, or at least tremendous luck, for wolf restoration to succeed if Congress barred the Fish and Wildlife Service and Park Service from releasing wolves in subsequent years.

Meanwhile, even as the transplanted wolves began exploring Yellowstone Park and the Idaho wilderness, the Wyoming Farm Bureau and the Sierra Club

Legal Defense Fund maintained their fight-to-the-death stand, seeking hearings in U.S. District Court. In an interesting twist of fate, a federal judge joined the two cases against government reintroduction plans, forcing the longtime enemies to work together. The legal system accomplished what the political system couldn't.

Although historians may view Yellowstone Park wolf restoration as an important conservation milestone, it's not a particularly good model for endangered species recovery. The process took too long, was unnecessarily divisive, and cost too much. The United States has hundreds of imperiled wildlife species in need of help. Unless we adopt new tactics, our nation's efforts to conserve endangered species will fail.

What's the solution? We need a process for resolving endangered species issues that brings people together instead of dividing them. We need leaders who will promote cooperation rather than confrontation. And we need interest groups—both industry and environmental—that truly want to find answers.

Paul Errington, in his classic book about predator-prey relationships, *Of Predation and Life*, observed: "Of all the native biological constituents of a northern wilderness scene, I should say that the wolves present the greatest test of human wisdom and good intentions."

Bringing wolves back to Yellowstone Park certainly shows our nation's good intentions. But the test of our wisdom will be whether we allow them to flourish.

1872	*Yellowstone National Park created by an act of Congress requiring preservation of its "natural curiosities, or wonders" and prohibiting "wanton destruction" of its fish and game. But hide hunters continue shooting thousands of elk and other ungulates and poisoning their carcasses to kill wolves and wolverines for pelts.*
1914	*Yellowstone wolf extirpation campaign begins after Congress appropriates funds for "destroying wolves, prairie dogs, and other animals injurious to agriculture and animal husbandry" on public lands—the start of a war against predators in the West.*
1926	*Two wolf pups are trapped on a bison carcass, the last of over one hundred thirty Yellowstone Park wolves killed in extirpation campaign begun in 1914.*
1935	*Yellowstone Park ends predator control in line with new National Park Service policy.*
1944	*Noted biologist Aldo Leopold advocates wolf restoration to Yellowstone ecosystem and other large western wild areas.*
1968	*Canadian wolf expert Douglas Pimlott in* Defenders *magazine advocates reintroducing wolves to Yellowstone Park and Canada's Banff and Jasper National Parks.*
1972	*President Nixon bans predator poisons on public lands. EPA extends curb to private lands.*
1973	*Congress enacts Endangered Species Act, mandating recovery planning for endangered and threatened species. Rocky Mountain gray wolf listed as endangered.*
1975	*Federal government forms Rocky Mountain wolf recovery team.*

1978	*In monograph written for Park Service, biologist John Weaver concludes that wolves no longer live in Yellowstone Park and recommends reintroduction.*
1980	*First Rocky Mountain wolf recovery plan drafted but doesn't make recommendation about Yellowstone Park. Conservationists urge reintroduction to park.*
1981	*Federal and state agencies begin revising recovery plan.*
1985	*Defenders of Wildlife sponsors Science Museum of Minnesota's* Wolves and Humans *exhibit in Yellowstone Park and Boise, Idaho. Over 215,000 park visitors see exhibit. Park Service Director William Mott backs Yellowstone Park wolf reintroduction. University of Montana survey finds overwhelming visitor support for Yellowstone Park wolf reintroduction.*
1986	*Wolf expert Dave Mech advocates Yellowstone Park reintroduction, calling the ecosystem "a place that literally begs to have wolves."*
1987	*Utah Democratic Representative Wayne Owens introduces legislation requiring immediate Yellowstone Park wolf reintroduction. U.S. Fish and Wildlife Service approves revised Rocky Mountain wolf recovery plan calling for reintroduction of wolves to the park.*
1988	*Congressman Owens says he's interested in "trying to restore a balance to Yellowstone National Park. The wolf is the only missing piece." Idaho Republican Senator Jim McClure backs Yellowstone Park and central Idaho wolf reintroduction if rancher interests are protected. Congress directs Park Service to study potential impacts of Yellowstone Park wolf reintroduction.*
1989	*Owens introduces legislation requiring government to prepare environmental impact statement on Yellowstone Park wolf reintroduction.*
1990	*Park Service publishes* Wolves for Yellowstone? *studies ordered by Congress. Defenders sets up $100,000 Wolf Compensation Fund. McClure introduces wolf reintroduction bill and holds*

hearing. Interior Secretary Manuel Lujan appoints Wolf Management Committee, charged with devising wolf reintroduction plan.

1991   *Wolf Management Committee submits recommendation to Congress; Congress ignores it. Congress votes funds for wolf EIS.*

1992   *First EIS hearings draw strong support from wolf advocates. Defenders sets up "Vote Wolf!" booth in Yellowstone Park to collect visitors' signatures. Congress directs agencies to finish EIS by January 1994.*

1993   *Draft Yellowstone Park wolf EIS released July 1. Public hearings draw mostly favorable comment. Defenders delivers over seventy thousand ballots, all but about two thousand pro-wolf, to secretary of the interior. Fish and Wildlife Service proposes starting Yellowstone Park and Idaho reintroduction in October 1994.*

1994   *Final EIS issued. On June 15, Interior Secretary Bruce Babbitt signs EIS record of decision. On November 22, Fish and Wildlife Service issues final rules for managing wolves reintroduced to Yellowstone Park and Idaho. On November 25, Wyoming Farm Bureau files suit against reintroduction plans, claiming "irreparable harm" to ranchers.*

1995   *On January 3, U.S. District Judge William Downes in Cheyenne, Wyoming, denies preliminary injunction sought by Wyoming Farm Bureau. On January 11, government begins shipping wild wolves from Alberta, Canada, but Farm Bureau wins temporary stay from federal appellate court in Denver, Colorado. On January 12, eight Canadian wolves arrive in Yellowstone Park. After appellate court lifts stay order, wolves are released into acclimation pens. On January 14, four wolves are released in Idaho's Frank Church-River of No Return Wilderness. On January 20, six more wolves reach Yellowstone Park and eleven more are released in Frank Church-River of No Return Wilderness. On March 21, Park Service begins releasing the fourteen Yellowstone Park wolves from acclimation pens.*

ACKNOWLEDGMENTS

Many people generously gave their time and counsel to make this book a reality. At the top of the list is Carol Woodruff, who not only edited the book but also took a personal interest in it. She provided insight and encouragement far beyond the call of duty. This book couldn't have been written without her commitment, and I'm deeply grateful.

I also owe special thanks to James G. Deane, editor of *Defenders* magazine, who reviewed the entire manuscript and contributed substantially to its accuracy and readability. My wife, Carol, has my gratitude and affection for her research, editorial assistance, and encouragement. My sons, Andy and Kit, showed a keen interest in this project and gave me help and support, which I appreciated. Now we can resume a normal life.

I owe a tremendous debt to the people who read all or most of the manuscript: John Varley, Brian Kahn, John Weaver, Dan Pletscher, Paul Schullery, and Steve Fritts. Their critical review improved this book significantly. My gratitude extends to those who reviewed specific chapters: Ed Bangs, Carter Niemeyer, Dave Mech, Doug Chadwick, Timm Kaminski, David Carr, Pat Tucker, Bruce Weide, Jerry Jack, and Tom France. Many thanks to all the people who helped find information and check facts.

I'd like to express my special thanks to Defenders of Wildlife and its board of directors for the support the organization has given me for the past seventeen years. I thank Rodger Schlickeisen, president of Defenders, for letting me forsake some of my normal duties while writing this book. I want to make clear that the opinions, perceptions, and perhaps errors contained in this book are my own—not Defenders'.

I apologize to all the important players in the Yellowstone Park wolf saga whom space, my editor, and readers' patience didn't permit me to mention. I regret that I couldn't give everyone the full recognition he or she deserves.

I'd like to acknowledge the exceptional contributions to Yellowstone Park wolf restoration made by Defenders staff members over the past twenty years, including Dick Randall, Cindy Shogan, James Deane, Ginger Meese, Rupert Cutler, Evan Hirsche, and Minette Johnson. Special thanks also are due Mollie Matteson and the volunteers from all over the nation who staffed the "Vote Wolf!" booth in Yellowstone Park for two summers. You made a difference.

I'd also like to acknowledge some of the important conservationists I was unable to mention in this book but who deserve recognition for their substantial contributions: Mike Roy, Carol Alette, and Steve Torbit of the National Wildlife Federation; Nick Lapham and Mollie Clayton of The Wolf Fund; Suzanne Laverty of the Wolf Recovery Foundation (now with The Wolf Education and Research Center); Michael Bean of the Environmental Defense Fund; Ed Lewis of the Greater Yellowstone Coalition; and Whit Tilt of the National Audubon Society (now with the National Fish and Wildlife Foundation).

I'd like to thank as well many of the key individuals and corporations that have supported Defenders' Yellowstone Park wolf work, especially Len and Sandy Sargent and Bob and Hopie Stevens. Thanks, too, to Patagonia, Inc.; Recreational Equipment, Inc.; the Larson Fund; and the Chase Foundation.

Many people in state and federal agencies have also played essential roles, among them Joe Fontaine, Carol Tenney, Dale Harms, Larry Shanks, and Kemper McMaster of the U.S. Fish and Wildlife Service; Norm Bishop, Marsha Karle, and Amy Vanderbilt of the National Park Service; and Jay Gore of the USDA Forest Service.

Finally, I'd like to acknowledge the consistent, accurate reporting on wolf recovery done by Dan Neal and Andrew Melnykovych of the Casper *Star-Tribune*; Rocky Barker of *The Post-Register*, in Idaho Falls; and Michael Milstein of the *Billings Gazette*. Thanks to the many other members of the media who did their job well—which means fairly.

It's impossible to thank everyone but discourteous not to try. To anyone I've accidentally omitted, I offer my sincere apology.

BIBLIOGRAPHY

Allen, Durward L. *Our Wildlife Legacy*. (Revised edition) New York: Funk & Wagnalls Co., 1962.

_____. *The Wolves of Minong: Their Vital Role in a Wild Community*. Boston: Houghton Mifflin, 1979.

Bailey, Vernon. *Animal Life of Yellowstone National Park*. Springfield, Baltimore: Charles C. Thomas, Publisher, 1930.

Bath, Alistair J., and Tom Buchanan. "Attitudes of Interest Groups in Wyoming Toward Wolf Restoration in Yellowstone National Park." *Wildlife Society Bulletin* 17 (1990): 519-525.

Bishop, Norman A. "Population Status of Large Mammals in Yellowstone National Park." Yellowstone-270 Leaflet, Yellowstone National Park (1989).

Brandenburg, Jim. *Brother Wolf: A Forgotten Promise*. Minocqua, WI: North Word Press, Inc., 1993.

Cahalane, Victor H. "The Evolution of Predator Control Policy in the National Parks." *Journal of Wildlife Management* 3 (July 1939): 229-237.

Carbyn, Ludwig N., ed. "Wolves in Canada and Alaska." Canadian Wildlife Service Report No. 45 (1983).

Chadwick, Douglas. "The Wolf's Song Returns to the North Fork." *Defenders* 59 (May/June 1984): 20-29.

_____. *The Kingdom: Wildlife in North America*. San Francisco: Sierra Club Books, 1990.

_____. "Manitoba's Wolves: A Model for Yellowstone." *Defenders* 62 (May/April 1987): 30-36.

_____. "Peril on the Border." *Defenders* 62 (July/August 1987): 10-11.

Chase, Alston. *Playing God in Yellowstone*. Boston, New York: The Atlantic Monthly Press, 1986.

Curnow, Edward. "The History of the Eradication of the Wolf in Montana." Master's thesis, University of Montana, 1969.

Cutler, M. Rupert. "Welcome the Wolf?" *Defenders* 63 (July/August 1988): 8-9, 29-30.

Despain, Don, Douglas Houston, Mary Meagher, and Paul Schullery. *Wildlife in Transition: Man and Nature on Yellowstone's Northern Range*. Boulder: Roberts Rinehart, Inc., 1986.

DeVoto, Bernard, ed. *The Journals of Lewis and Clark*. Boston: Houghton Mifflin Company, 1953.

Dunlop, Thomas R. *Saving America's Wildlife*. Princeton: Princeton University Press, 1988.

Errington, Paul L. *Of Predation and Life*. Ames: Iowa State University Press, 1967.

Fischer, Hank. "Can Western Wolves Make a Comeback?" *Defenders* 59 (May/June 1984): 30-32.

_____. "Wolves and Yellowstone." *Defenders* 60 (July/August 1985): 38-39.

_____. "David Mech Discusses the Wolf." *Defenders* 61 (November/December 1986): 6-15.

_____. "Deep Freeze for Wolf Recovery?" *Defenders* 62 (November/December 1987): 28-33.

_____. "Wolves for Yellowstone?" *Defenders* 63 (March/April 1988): 16-17.

_____. "Discord Over Wolves." *Defenders* 66 (July/August 1991): 35-39.

_____. "Wolves for Yellowstone." *Defenders* 68 (summer 1993): 12-17.

Flader, Susan. *Thinking Like a Mountain.* Columbia: University of Missouri Press, 1974.

Fritts, Steven H. "Wolf Depredation on Livestock in Minnesota." U.S. Fish and Wildlife Service Resource Publication 145, Washington, D.C., 1982.

Fritts, Steven H., and L. David Mech. "Movements of Translocated Wolves in Minnesota." *Journal of Wildlife Management* 48 (1984): 709-721.

Fox, Michael W., ed. *The Wild Canids.* New York: Van Nostrand Reinhold Co., 1975.

Kaminski, Timm J., and Jerome Hansen. "The Wolves of Central Idaho." Montana Cooperative Wildlife Research Unit, Missoula, 1984.

Kellert, Stephen R. "The Public and the Timber Wolf in Minnesota." Paper. New Haven: Yale School of Forestry and Environmental Studies, 1985.

Leopold, Aldo. *Game Management.* New York: Charles Scribner's Sons, 1933.

_____. "Review of *The Wolves of North America*, by S. P. Young and E. A. Goldman, 1944." *Journal of Forestry* 42 (1944): 928-929.

_____. *A Sand County Almanac.* New York: Oxford University Press, Inc., 1949.

Lopez, Barry H. *Of Wolves and Men.* New York: Charles Scribner's Sons, 1978.

McNamee, Thomas. "Yellowstone's Missing Wolves." *Defenders* 67 (November/December 1992): 24-31.

McNaught, David. "Wolves in Yellowstone Park? Park Visitors Respond." *Wildlife Society Bulletin* 15 (1987): 518-521.

Mech, L. David. "The Wolves of Isle Royale." U.S. Department of the Interior, National Park Service Fauna Series 7. Government Printing Office, Washington, D.C., 1986.

_____. *The Wolf: The Ecology and Behavior of an Endangered Species.* Garden City, New York: The Natural History Press, 1970.

_____. "Meet the Wolf." *Defenders* 66 (November/December 1991): 28-32.

_____. *The Way of the Wolf.* Stillwater, MN: Voyageur Press, Inc., 1991.

Mowat, Farley. *Never Cry Wolf.* New York: Dell Publishing Co., Inc., 1963.

Murie, Adolph. "The Wolves of Mount McKinley." U.S. Department of the Interior, National Park Service Fauna Series 5. Government Printing Office, Washington, D.C., 1944.

_____. *A Naturalist in Alaska.* New York: Doubleday & Co., Inc., 1963.

_____. "Ecology of the Coyote in the Yellowstone." U.S. Department of Agriculture Fauna Series 5. Government Printing Office, Washington, D.C., 1940.

Murie, Olaus J. "Food Habits of the Coyote in Jackson Hole, Wyoming." U.S. Department of Agriculture Circular 362. Government Printing Office, Washington, D.C., 1935.

Pimlott, Douglas H. "The Use of Tape-Recorded Wolf Howls to Locate Timber Wolves." Paper presented at the 22nd Midwest Wildlife Conference, 1960.

_____. "Wolf Control in Canada." *Canadian Audubon Magazine* (November-December 1961): 145-52.

_____. "Review of F. Mowat's *Never Cry Wolf.*" *Journal of Wildlife Management* 30 (1966): 236-37.

_____. "Wolves and Men in North America." *Defenders of Wildlife News* 42 (1967): 36-53.

Pimlott, Douglas H., John A. Shannon, and George B. Kolenosky. "The Ecology of the Timber Wolf in Algonquin Park." Ontario Department of Lands and Forests, 1969.

Randall, Dick. "Wolves for Yellowstone." *Defenders* 55 (June 1980): 188-190.

Ream, Robert R. "Wolf Ecology Project Annual Report, 1984-1985." Montana Fish, Wildlife and Parks Department Project SE-1-7, 1985.

Rutter, Russell J., and Douglas H. Pimlott. *The World of the Wolf.* Philadelphia and New York: J. B. Lippincott Co., 1968.

Singer, Francis. "The History and Status of Wolves in Glacier National Park, Montana." Glacier National Park Scientific Paper 1, 1975.

_____. "The Ungulate Prey Base for Large Predators in Yellowstone National Park." Research/Resources Management Report No. 1. Washington, D.C.: National Park Service, 1988.

U.S. Fish and Wildlife Service. "Northern Rocky Mountain Wolf Recovery Plan." U.S. Department of the Interior, Fish and Wildlife Service, 1980.

_____. "Northern Rocky Mountain Wolf Recovery Plan." Denver: U.S. Department of the Interior, Fish and Wildlife Service, 1987.

_____. "Interim Wolf Control Plan. Northern Rocky Mountains of Montana and Wyoming." Denver: U.S. Department of the Interior, Fish and Wildlife Service, 1988.

Weaver, John L. "The Wolves of Yellowstone." U.S. National Park Service, Natural Resource Report No. 14, Government Printing Office, Washington, D.C., 1978.

_____. "Of Wolves and Livestock." *Western Wildlands* 8 (winter 1983): 37-39.

_____. "Ecology of Wolf Predation Amidst High Ungulate Diversity in Jasper National Park, Alberta." Ph.D. dissertation, University of Montana, 1994.

Wilson, Edward O. *Biophilia.* Cambridge: Harvard University Press, 1984.

Wolf Management Committee. "Reintroduction and Management of Wolves in Yellowstone National Park and the Central Idaho Wilderness Area." Report to the United States Congress. U.S. Fish and Wildlife Service unpublished report, 1991.

"Who's Afraid of the Big Bad Wolf?" *Audubon* 92 (March 1990): 82-85.

Wolves in American Culture Committee, ed. *Wolf.* Ashland, WI: North Word Press, Inc., 1986.

Young, Stanley P. "The War on the Wolf." *American Forests* 48 (November 1942): 492-495, 526.

_____. "The War on the Wolf." *American Forests* 48 (December 1942): 552-555, 572-574.

Young, Stanley P., and Edward A. Goldman. *The Wolves of North America: Part I.* New York: Dover Publications, Inc., 1944.

_____. *The Wolves of North America: Part II.* New York: Dover Publications, Inc., 1944.

INDEX

H A N K   F I S C H E R

Hank Fischer has covered the Northern Rockies Region (Montana, Idaho, Wyoming) for Defenders of Wildlife since 1977. His office is in Missoula, Montana; he has worked in a professional position for a national conservation organization longer than anyone else in this region.

He has been intensively involved with endangered species recovery issues, particularly those involving wolves, grizzly bears and black-footed ferrets. He developed Defenders' Wolf Compensation Fund, which uses private money to reimburse ranchers for verified livestock losses to wolves. He was the project director for Defenders' 1993 publication, *Building Economic Incentives into the Endangered Species Act.*

Fischer has also been involved with a variety of national forest issues and has been active in national wildlife refuge management. He was instrumental in the creation of statewide wildlife viewing systems for Montana and Idaho, and is co-author of the *Montana Wildlife Viewing Guide* (Falcon Press, 1990).

He holds a Master of Science degree in Environmental Studies from the University of Montana, where he studied wildlife biology and journalism. His undergraduate degree is from Ohio University. He is the author of dozens of articles on natural resource topics and is a regular commentator on Montana public radio.

He has won numerous awards, including the National Resources Council of America's Award of Achievement for Education for bringing the *Wolves and Humans* exhibit to Yellowstone National Park and Boise, Idaho, in 1986; a National Environmental Awards Council Special Merit Award for creating Defenders of Wildlife's Wolf Compensation Fund in 1990; and a Regional Forester Award from the Northern Region of the Forest Service for developing the *Montana Wildlife Viewing Guide* in 1991. Most recently, he was the recipient of the 1993 Don Aldrich Fish, Wildlife and Conservation Award.

183

RESTORING THE WOLF TO
YELLOWSTONE NATIONAL PARK
DEFENDERS OF WILDLIFE

POSTER SIZE: 23 x 32¹/₂"
PRICE: $25.00

Restoring the Wolf to Yellowstone

T*he Rocky Mountain Wolf was the only species missing from the Yellowstone National Park area. Celebrate its return with this compelling colorful, art-quality poster by Montana artist Monte Dolack.*

P*art of the proceeds from the sale of this poster goes to The Wolf Compensation Fund, a special fund created and managed by Defenders of Wildlife to compensate ranchers for livestock losses and shift economic responsibility to the millions of people who want to see wolf populations restored.*

To order this poster or a free catalog of outdoor recreational guidebooks and nature gift ideas call 1-800-582-2665.

FALCON™